PUBLISH

TAKE CHARGE OF YOUR AUTHOR CAREER

Second Edition

PUBLISH

TAKE CHARGE
OF YOUR
AUTHOR
CAREER

G.C. Boris & M. Haskell

Ordering Information:

Quantity sales. Special discounts are available on quantity purchases by corporations, associations, and others. For details, contact the publisher at the address above.

Cover Design by Michelle Fairbanks

Edited by Kimberly Peticolas

Interior Design and E-book Formatting by Kimberly Peticolas

Paperback: 978-0-9994354-4-1

E-Book: 978-0-9994354-5-8

Second Edition

Table of Contents

Dedicated to DeAnna Cameron and the O.C. Writers Community for challenging and inspiring us to write this book.

Introduction

Many people in the publishing industry have strong opinions about the right and the wrong ways to bring a book to market. They base their opinions on their personal experiences, what's worked for them, and what hasn't. They believe that if it worked for them, it will work for you.

But they don't know you.

What makes this book different is that we believe there is no single correct path to publication. Why? Because we're all unique. We each have different strengths, weaknesses, and motivations. One writer is no more important than another, regardless of their paycheck.

Knowing where you fit on the author spectrum will not only help you design your version of success, but will also give you the tools to get there. When you identify your author personality type and understand which publishing paths are best for you, you'll also be able to move from one type to another if you choose. When you know where you are, you can create a path to where you want to be.

We've divided the writing world into five basic personality types: the artist, the bucket-lister, the calling-card writer, the dabbler, and the entrepreneur. Rather than viewing these types as set and immovable, we see them as a continuum.

Megan and Greta are perfect examples of this. While they both started out as dabblers and eventually became artist-entrepreneurs, their journeys were very different.

Megan began writing to pass the time on the train as she commuted to a job as a forensic accountant. She was a quantitative analyst who found diversion in fantasy.

Eventually she decided to try her hand at writing a full-length novel. It took four years and several false starts to finish that manuscript. She sent it to a few friends and family members and held her breath. The responses finally came. "It's good . . . but . . ." In other words, it needed to be scrapped and buried in a deep dark filing cabinet.

Not being one to give up easily, she studied, worked on her craft, and wrote another book she believed was publishable. To be sure, she pitched it to editors and agents at a local writers' conference and got some really positive feedback.

However, Megan's work experience had given her an appetite for business. She loved the idea of starting her own imprint and managing her book through the publishing process. That manuscript ultimately became an award-winning book and the first in her popular series, The Sanyare Chronicles.

Greta started her writing life in the magazine industry. She sold advertising, was the production manager for two national books, and finally became a contract writer. Consequently, she wrote nonfiction. It wasn't until she interviewed two fiction authors for a magazine article that she realized writing a novel was a possibility.

Coming from a traditional publishing background, that was the way she chose to go. Countless stories and countless rejections later, she signed a deal for her Seven Deadly Sins series with a small publishing house.

Both Greta and Megan bring their unique perspectives to this book and to the online course that accompanies it. (You can find more about that at www.AuthorWheel.com/

PublishCourse.) While they have many differences, they have one critical thing in common—their love of books.

In her early years, Nancy Drew's careful choice of sleuthing outfits made Greta aware of the importance of dressing for success. In her teens, Shakespeare's wandering forest fairies caused her to ponder man's position in the universe. Poe's secret in the chimney introduced her to insomnia. Peter Benchley's *Jaws* ruined her for ocean swimming.

When Megan's father handed her a battered old copy of *The Hobbit* at the young age of ten or eleven, he didn't realize he was spawning his own book-hoarding dragon. *Pride and Prejudice* taught her that first impressions aren't always accurate. And her dissection of *Frankenstein* in college English Literature provided proof that the monster isn't always the guy with the scars.

From the days when Greta and Megan's parents tucked them in at night with a bedtime story to present day, literature has played a powerful role in each of their lives. Books and stories transport them, mesmerize them, and make them thoughtful adults. Books alter their worldview and regularly burn through their stubborn perceptions of reality.

We want more books in the world.

Since tackling the writing process, we now know that those who pen the tales don't have things as easy as their readers. Writing is hard work, and the publishing process is even harder. Writers who put fingers to keyboard and make their mental meanderings, wonder-ings, and what-if-ings public are some of the bravest people around.

Through this book, we hope to inspire you to find that courage and start your author career. We want to read what you think about the universe and elves and end times and healthy eating and dragons and serial killers and the girl next door.

We hope you join us and start your publishing journey today.

Chapter One
Your Author Personality

At The Author Wheel, we believe there's no single right way to produce, publish, or promote your books, only the best ways for you and your projects. This belief forms the core of all of our classes. The hard part is cutting through the online noise to understand yourself, your options, and ultimately your next steps. That's why we're here to help.

We've been teaching workshops and classes on the various publishing paths at conferences and local events since 2017. During that time, we realized that many new writers, and even some experienced ones, hadn't taken the time to examine their present position, motivations, or vision for their writing life. In fact, we hadn't fully examined ourselves.

This lack of self-knowledge puts people at a disadvantage. We met people who'd penned a memoir about a painful divorce or their personal journey after the death of their child, who were planning to pitch their books to agents and publishers. These people weren't celebrities or doctors, just individuals who desired to share their story with friends and family, and hopefully help a few others along the way. They didn't want to go on book tours or build a career from the work, but they had a story to tell. We didn't think the agented traditional route was going to be a good choice for them, but it was hard to explain why.

We also met people who took years to polish and perfect their literary novel and dreamed of major book awards, but then planned to independently publish because they'd heard it was the only way to make any money with their writing. The problem was, many of those big book awards aren't open to self-published titles, and literary works can be difficult to market without the resources of a big publisher. Their goals didn't align with their planned path to publication.

Yet in our courses, we were presenting generic material about the publishing industry, and the only way we could guide these people who had different goals and needs was on an individual level. That doesn't work very well when you have fifty people in a class and ten minutes for Q&A.

This got us thinking: If we could come up with a way for people to evaluate themselves, it would be a lot easier to steer them toward the material that would help them most.

That's where the Author Personality Quiz comes in. If you haven't taken it yet, it's available for free on The Author Wheel website (www.authorwheel.com).

The personality quiz separates writers into five categories: the artist, the bucket-lister, the calling-card writer, the dabbler, and the entrepreneur. As with any personality quiz, you may fall into more than one type. You could be, like both of us, a balance between the entrepreneur and the artist. You could be a dabbler who wants to become an entrepreneur.

The quiz isn't meant to pigeonhole you, but to give you a starting point. If you've been writing and publishing for a while, you also may find your author personality changes over time. For you, the quiz could help you better understand your current goals and motivations, and be a refresher or a reset.

For each of the personalities, we've identified the publication journey that is best aligned for that personality's goals. However, we'll discuss those paths in more detail in the next chapter. For now, you just need to know that we've divided the publishing world into three primary paths to publication: agented traditional, small press traditional, and independent publishing (a.k.a. self-publishing). Although there are many ways to categorize the publishing industry, we believe these are the most common.

Which personality are you?

THE ARTIST

It's all about the craft for the artist. Of course you'd like to make money, who wouldn't? But your primary goal is to put beautiful prose on the page and to be recognized for your hard work and creativity. You may feel it's not your job to be involved in the business end of things, or that marketing is completely outside your skill set.

If the quiz proclaimed you an artist, it doesn't mean you're an amazing writer right now. It does mean it is more important to you to craft wonderful stories than to make a quick buck.

For many artists, the choice to work with a traditional publishing house is good. Publishers often offer opportunities to work with a high caliber editor and production team. And, because it's so difficult nowadays to get a publishing contract, you will have to spend a lot of time perfecting your writing skills up front. Newer writers especially will learn a lot from this process.

And if accolades and prestigious book awards are a goal for you, traditional publishing is often the only way to get them.

However, some artists also see publishing and marketing as an art. Maybe you're also interested in the business side of publishing. If that's the case, studying the art of storytelling is still something you should pursue. Taking classes and attending writers' conferences should still be top priorities. But you might also explore the world of independent publishing.

It depends on your mindset and how long you're willing to wait to see your book in print.

For example, when Megan took the test, she was almost 50/50 Artist and Entrepreneur. However, she never even considered a traditional contract because she wanted to run her own business. She looked forward to learning the ins and outs of publishing as much as creating powerful stories that would resonate with readers for years to come. So even though she identified as the artist, she chose the independent publishing route.

It turned out Greta's personality was the same, but where Megan chose the independent path, Greta pursued a contract with a boutique press. For her, the business and marketing side of the industry was intimidating. She wanted a partner to walk her through the process and help her bring her series to life. Plus, having someone else financially invest in her work gave her the confidence she needed to move forward.

That said, there are also opportunities to pursue both paths. Many of our independent author friends are also pursuing traditional publishing deals in order to reach readers in different markets. Sometimes this is for specific mediums (like audiobooks only), or for specific genres that may sell better with the backing of a big publishing house, or because they want to try it and see what happens.

The benefit of the modern publishing industry is that it's flexible and diverse! There are markets and paths for every niche. So once you understand yourself and your goals, you can find the path that works for your life.

THE BUCKET-LISTER

The bucket-lister has a book burning a hole in their computer. Whether it's their personal memoir or a unique how-to for a small niche market, they want to get that manuscript off their hard drive and into the world before they die. Most bucket-listers have never had a strong desire to be a writer. It's the message of the one book that motivates them, not a career in writing.

Generally, these kinds of books don't attract a traditional publisher and are better suited for independent publishing. Writing technique and a large built-in audience are things publishers look for. If you have neither, it will be tough to get a deal. This typically leaves independent publishing as a bucket-lister's best option.

However, if you're a bucket-lister, you need to consider the cost of publication. How badly do you want to see your book in print?

Understand that while writing may be an art, publishing is a business. Like any other business, there are costs involved in both time and money. Many writers don't realize they can't simply "put their book up on Amazon." There are multiple steps involved in that process including setting up an author account which will require basic business information like social security numbers, bank account numbers, and your physical address. Even if you want to give your book away for free, Amazon will still require this information before they list your book on the site.

Your book will be available to the public as a representation of you. You're going to want to make sure you're proud of your product. Which means you're probably going to need some professional help to get it there. Unless you have a friend or family member who's an editor, you must pay for that help.

Now, as you go through the process of writing your book and getting it ready for publication, you may get bit by the writing bug. That's terrific! However, if you only want to publish that one book, and find the entire process overwhelming, you might decide to pay a reputable book coach or hybrid publishing company to help you.

But beware: there are many dishonest people and companies

who will promise great things for your book, take your money, and deliver very little. If a 'publisher' asks for money upfront, they are not a traditional press. Make sure you read the contracts carefully. We'll talk more about these companies in the next chapter on the various publishing paths.

THE CALLING-CARD WRITER

The calling-card writer's primary motive for writing a book is the business behind the book. Whether your goal is to speak, teach, or promote your services, a book can lend credibility to your career.

The difference between the calling-card writer and the entrepreneur may seem slight, but it isn't. While both are business-minded, the calling-card writer's primary goal *isn't* to be a writer. They already have a business unrelated to writing, or are focused on building one. Their goal is to establish themselves as experts in their field. In fact, the books themselves may or may not make money, because that's not their primary purpose.

For example, there are many doctors who have published New York Times bestselling books on diet and nutrition. They don't stop seeing patients, touring, or speaking. The books, even radically successful ones, support their existing platform. In fact, many of them are written by ghostwriters, and not the author whose name is on the cover.

Calling-card writers typically prefer the faster independent path to publication because they're not looking for distribution into libraries and bookstores, or those elusive big-name awards. They want to get their book to their clients or customers as quickly as possible. Most times, they plan to give paperback copies away free as a marketing tactic.

However it's important to note that it can sometimes be easier to get an agent and a publisher for a nonfiction book, so if you have a big practice, celebrity connections, a very large mailing list, or a unique take on a popular subject, pursuing a traditional publishing deal could be a good direction for you.

Ultimately, the decision whether to publish yourself or to seek a traditional deal is going to rest on your goals for the book. If you need the book sooner rather than later, independent publishing is the only path that will give you control over your publication date. If you're less concerned with speed to market, more concerned with prestige and believe you have the clout to attract a traditional deal, go for it.

THE DABBLER

The dabbler has a lot of ideas. Knowing which ones to pursue and how to pursue them is their quandary. We love dabblers. Many well-known, successful authors began that way. Since most dabblers are just sticking their toes in the writing waters, it's important for them to understand what's beneath the surface.

There are different kinds of writing careers and each comes with its own difficulties, pros, and cons. When Greta first started writing, she wrote articles for magazines. Then she moved on to write and independently publish a self-help book. Then she edited an online magazine. For several years, it seemed like this nonfiction work was her best path forward, but she had an itch to write a thriller. She did, found a publisher, and shifted her focus to fiction. However, when she was offered the opportunity to lead the OC Writers community, she returned to her nonfiction routes and began writing blog posts for writers.

Greta has written fiction and nonfiction, published in magazines, edited magazines, self-published, and gotten a seven-book traditional contract. Although she was a dabbler for many years, that journey has helped her become a better writer and refine her writing and publishing goals.

The key is, she finished the projects she started. Most of them, anyway. She didn't allow the lure of the bright new shiny thing to draw her away from her goals of the moment. She set her mind to one project at a time. When she'd completed it, she reevaluated, chose the next thing and learned from that.

It's difficult to recommend a path to publication for a dabbler, because it depends on which of your fifty projects we're talking about. If you're having fun writing short stories, submitting them to journals or multi-author anthologies is a great way to go. If you're writing nonfiction articles, you'll want to find publications that feature your subject-matter. Starting a blog can also be a great way to "find yourself" as a writer.

Full-length books are more of a commitment. They take longer to write, and they're harder to publish. Unless you're committed to the process, the dabbler may find a novel to be practically impossible to finish. For that reason, it may make sense to start with shorter things and work your way up the word count ladder.

Regardless of what you choose, if you want to save yourself years of floundering around, we suggest picking one project, writing it, aiming for publication, then evaluating your experience. Did it scratch your itch? Or are you now ready to take what you learned and try something else?

THE ENTREPRENEUR

We finally come to the type of writer that most writing blogs, podcasts and websites target: the entrepreneur.

The entrepreneur's primary goal is to have a financially lucrative writing career. You want to earn an income from your books. To do this, you must be self-motivated, flexible, experimental, have leadership skills, and be willing to put in the hours. Entrepreneurs are lifetime learners.

Your choice of independent or traditional publication will have more to do with the particular project you're releasing than any set opinion or industry bias. In fact, many business-minded authors do both.

You'll find as you search the net that there are a lot of strong opinions. Some people believe independent publishing is ruining the industry through unprofessional products and cheap prices. They believe that if you can't attract an agent, you're not yet good enough to be published, even though getting an agent and a publishing contract has as much to do with the market as it does with the quality of your writing.

Meanwhile, there's a loud contingent on the other side that believes the traditional model is a good ole boys (and girls) club that takes advantage of authors and gives them ego strokes instead of an income. Advances are shrinking and the publishers' marketing efforts are dwindling. Traditional publishers might put your book in bookstores and libraries, but many of those outlets are closing up shop as e-books and online retailers gain ground. These indie proponents think you're more likely to become financially successful and earn a full-time income if you publish the book yourself.

We've said it before and we'll say it again: there's no single right way to publish your book.

The entrepreneur should be less concerned with the politics of publishing and more with the production of outstanding books. Your goal is to earn an income from your writing, which requires developing a fan base of readers. To do that, you need a high-quality product, and you also must learn the industry.

The key for the entrepreneur is to take the time to design a career you believe will work for you, your writing style and speed, your skill set, and, honestly, your passion. Passion is one of the few things that will help you through a disappointing book launch and almost all career authors have them.

Now that you know where you are on the author

spectrum—or where you want to be—it's time to take charge of your author career.

TO RECAP

We've divided the author community into five personality types. You can take a free quiz at http://AuthorWheel.com to find out where you fall on the spectrum.

Our recommendations for the Artist are:
Study craft and story structure

- Attend conferences and join writers' organizations
- Write and publish shorter works in your genre to build a portfolio
- Create a professional website
- Start an email list
- Choose one or two social media platforms and create professional pages there

Our recommendations for the Bucket-Lister are:
Set a publishing budget

- Learn about the independent publishing process
- Research reputable book coaches/hybrid publishers

Our recommendations for the Calling-Card Writer are:
Evaluate your publishing goals

- Evaluate your current platform
- Learn about your publishing options based on the above
- Add a landing page about the book to your business website
- Start a blog and/or newsletter on the topic of the book

- Begin posting on this topic on your current business related social media platforms

Our recommendations for the Dabbler are:

- Learn as much as you can about the various arms of the publishing industry.
- Check out Duotrope to see what different publishers are looking for
- Attend a writers' conference and/or join a writers' group
- Pick a project and see it all the way through publication
- Create a website if you don't have one
- Start a blog

Our recommendations for the Entrepreneur are:

- Create a career mission statement
- Study writing craft
- Attend conferences and join writers' groups
- Learn about the publishing industry
- Create a professional website
- Start an email list
- Choose one or two social media platforms and create professional pages there

Chapter Two
A Publishing Overview

There are many ways to publish a book. You can try to get an agent and a deal with a big publishing house. You can seek a smaller press that doesn't require the agent middleman. You can pay a hybrid publisher, a book coach, or a vanity press to get your book out. You can independently publish by setting up your own imprint, or you can upload files to Amazon and select them as your publisher of record.

In the author community there are a lot of strong opinions about which of these options is best. Many people believe that the traditional model is the only professional one, and that independent publishing is ruining the industry with amateurish books and cheap pricing. Others believe traditional publishing is antiquated, slow, and takes advantage of authors who could be more financially successful on their own. We know very successful authors on both sides of the issue.

The truth is, every author will have their own definition of success because every author has a different reason for writing. We each have unique personalities, strengths, weaknesses, and vision. The goal of this book is to teach you about your options so you can make an educated choice that will help you achieve your personal goals.

In this chapter, we give you an overview of the three most common paths to publication: traditional agented, traditional boutique or small press, and independent or self-publishing. Keep in mind, as we cover these segments of the industry, we're not going in depth on the subject of marketing. This is because marketing is an extremely variable topic.

In the past, publishers were responsible for all the marketing and promotions not only for an author's books, but for the author themselves. If the author is a celebrity, or has proven themselves in some way, this may still be true. Most of the time it isn't. Your distaste for marketing shouldn't determine your path to publication. Whether you are traditionally or independently published, marketing and promotions will be a part of your life if you want to sell books.

We realize this isn't a popular opinion. You will find authors who disagree, authors whose book took off thanks to their publisher's fantastic promotions. In our experience, while this is always possible, it isn't the norm. Hence the subtitle of the book—take charge of your author career.

As you read this chapter, we suggest you keep an open mind. Your publishing journey should be uniquely tailored to you, your project, and your overall goals. So let's talk about the first path—traditional agented.

TRADITIONAL AGENTED PATH

In this model, the author is looking for an agent to represent them in negotiating a book contract. In practical terms, this means you would first query book agents who might be interested in your work. If they like your query, they may ask you to send them a sample of your manuscript, usually the first fifty pages or the full manuscript for fiction or a formal outline and synopsis for nonfiction. If they fall in love with your book or concept, they'll offer to represent you for a percentage of your future advance and book royalties—once they pitch and find a publisher.

The fact is, many of the big publishers won't even look at your manuscript without an agent's representation. Large publishers don't have time to sift through the thousands and thousands of manuscripts written each year. If they did, they'd never have time to produce and market books. Agents become their filter. They're like the gold miners of the old west. They sift through the sand and bring in the gems. A good, experienced agent will have solid relationships with acquisitions editors and a reputation for picking manuscripts that sell well in the market.

A seasoned agent can also act as a mentor and will help their authors navigate the publishing industry. They know what publishers are looking for. They understand book contracts and may be able to negotiate a better deal—perhaps a bigger advance or better terms than what the publisher would offer an author on their own. They've seen the kinds of books that get big deals, and the kinds that don't. And finally, some agents will also work to sell foreign, audio, and film rights for your book.

An agent only gets paid when you do, so it's in their interest to help you maximize your writing income.

However, as with anything, there are also disadvantages to signing with an agent. Foremost, it can take a very, very long time to attract one. Some believe that because of the current economic climate and the rise of subscription TV services, this is getting worse. It may be.

If you go this route, prepare for rejection and lots of it. It can be discouraging. Steven King, J. K. Rowling, John Grisham—just to name a few of the greats—were rejected by agents and/or publishing houses many, many times. Seeking an agent takes a thick skin, persistence, and patience.

Speaking of patience, when you get an agent, it can also take them a long, long time to sell your manuscript to a publisher.

And when, or if, they sell your book to a publisher, the timeline from purchase to print for the large houses is also very long—a year and a half to two years is common. Do the math. It's not unusual for people to wait seven to ten years to see their book in print, and the book that's finally published may not be the one they started out with.

Another disadvantage to seeking an agent is the expense. Often the only way you can get their attention is by showing up at writers' conferences and paying an additional fee on top of the registration fee for a private meeting. And when, or if, you sell a book through an agent, you'll have to share any money you make with them.

If pitching agents sounds overwhelming and exhausting, but you'd still like a traditional deal, don't despair. There are boutique presses out there that don't require a middleman.

TRADITIONAL BOUTIQUE PATH

The second publishing option is to pitch directly to one of the many smaller boutique houses that don't require an agent as a go-between. Often these publishers are new and don't have the track record to tempt agents, or they are genre specific. For instance, they may only publish cozy mysteries, or romance, or they are an e-book only press.

The advantage to working with a small boutique press, as stated, is that you don't have to have an agent or middleman to pitch to them, which saves time and money. That's how Greta got her deal. When her publisher was new, they accepted unsolicited manuscripts from authors without an agent. Greta pitched them directly, and they were so excited about her series, they signed her for a two-book deal with the right of first refusal on the rest of the seven-book series. With a small press, that's far more likely to happen than with a big house.

Another significant benefit of a boutique press is that they're hungry for new titles and more willing to strike deals more favorable to the author. This means that your royalty split is generally larger than it would be with a big press, and if you don't have an agent, you don't have to share that money with anybody.

You will also get many of the same production advantages as you would with a large press: experienced editors, cover designers, and formatters. But you also often have more input in production decisions, like your front cover, and their publishing schedule is usually more open, so the time to get your book to market is shorter.

Small presses sound pretty great, don't they? Unfortunately, there is always another side to every coin. Small presses don't have the clout, public relations systems, or marketing budgets of the large houses, so it's more difficult to get your books into libraries and bookstores. This means you'll typically sell fewer copies in the first few months after launch.

In addition, small publishers may not enter your books into prestigious awards contests, because most of them cost money. And professional review services like Kirkus and Library Digest rarely take them seriously.

One other consideration is that many of them won't offer an advance, or if they do, it will be small. We've heard that this is becoming a common practice at the big publishing houses for debut authors, but with a small press it's almost guaranteed. Remember, they are small businesses, often just starting out, and they won't have the capital to spend up front. Of course, this is offset by the benefit that they will typically offer higher royalty splits after the book launch as compared to the big publishers.

A Point of Clarity: Boutique publishers should not be confused with hybrid publishers or "vanity" presses. These companies help you publish your work for a fee. Some of them are reputable, some aren't, but they are associated with the independent publishing model, not the traditional one.

Traditional boutique publishing houses go through the same selection process as their larger counterparts, but publish a smaller number of titles each year. They never charge you money or require that you purchase books or other services from them. They assume all the costs related to book production and advertising and pay you an advance or royalties when the book makes money.

INDEPENDENT PATH

For this book, we use the terms 'independent publishing,' 'indie,' and 'self-publishing' synonymously. That said, we prefer the term independent publishing over self-publishing because even if they're doing the work themselves, a nontraditional author is acting as their own publishing house. They do all the things a traditional press does except acquisitions, though the degree of professionalism and financial investment may depend on whether the author is looking for a career or a hobby.

This means the limits of the independent author correspond to their own network and ability (or desire) to think and act like an entrepreneur. For example, you'll need to find and hire your own team—editors, cover designers, formatters, etc.—and you'll make every decision on the marketing of your book, from retail price to advertising and promotions.

To produce a high-quality product—a book that is for all intents and purposes indistinguishable from anything you'd find in the bookstore—you can't do everything on your own. In fact, Megan hires at least four people—in recent years more—to assist her in various aspects of book production, from cover designers and artists to editors and virtual assistants. She acts as her own publisher. She may be independent from the traditional publishing houses, but she's still striving for the same quality.

Not everyone who writes a book will want to make a career of it. If you're a bucket-lister, for example, you may only want to publish one book for posterity or as a passion project. These projects may not warrant a big expenditure or a team. And often indie authors who are just starting out don't have a lot of cash to invest. In later chapters, we'll discuss ways to reduce costs while still achieving a high-quality product.

There are some serious advantages to being an indie author. For one thing, you'll earn the highest possible royalty per book sold. For example, on Amazon, you'll earn 70% of the retail price of every e-book priced between $2.99 and $9.99. Even if you sell fewer books than the traditionally published authors, you may end up making more total income. It's all a numbers game.

Indies can also get their books into the hands of readers much sooner than those who publish through the traditional model because they don't have to rely on committees for approvals or over-burdened editors. If you write fast, this can be an immense game changer because the more books you publish, the more potential income you can earn. We have friends who write and publish five or more books a year.

You can also move faster to meet market demand and pivot your strategy when necessary. If the cover isn't working, get a new one. If you think your price is too high, lower it. Traditional publishing houses can't be as nimble.

And, as an indie, you have full control over every aspect of your book, which is perfect for those who are type A. No one else will decide if your book has been edited enough. No one else will choose your cover or force you to accept something you don't like.

Unfortunately, that's also one of the major drawbacks. If every decision is your responsibility, there's no one else to blame if things go wrong.

Being indie also means you have the hardest time selling to bookstores and libraries. You simply won't have the connections—at least not on a national level. Big organizations are unlikely to buy books from unknown authors. You may be able to talk your way into the local library or your favorite indie bookstore, but it's usually not a strategy worth pursuing beyond that. So if it's important to see your book on a shelf at the airport, the indie path is probably not for you.

Similarly, the big prestigious awards are typically not open to indie authors. Most will only take submissions from the major publishers or nominations from big name traditional authors. That's changing a bit, but independently published authors are still a long way from full acceptance by the traditional branch of the industry.

Indies will also need to have cash on hand to invest in their work. It doesn't have to be thousands of dollars, but even bucket-listers should budget a few hundred. We'll talk more about costs later.

Last, the indie path requires organization and self-motivation. Even if you don't want to be an entrepreneur, or are just publishing for fun, you will need the internal drive to reach the finish line. Your deadlines are your own, so it's up to you to keep to them.

HYBRID AUTHORS

Many authors find they have different goals for different projects. One manuscript may be better suited for one publishing path and another a different path. Enter the hybrid author.

We know many authors who have started out with a traditional publishing deal and then have either taken back their rights and self-published their backlist, or written a second series with the direct purpose of publishing independently. Greta is planning to independently publish a new series at the writing of this book. Other authors begin with the independent model, then decide they want to pursue the wider reach of the traditional houses.

Why would they do this? Because, as we've noted, both traditional and indie paths have advantages and disadvantages. By publishing different projects in different ways, an author is able to get the advantages of both.

So don't think that if you publish your first book as an indie you'll never get a traditional deal, or if you publish with a big house, you're stuck there forever. However, be sure to check your contract if you sign with a publisher. It isn't wise to sell your rights to all your books forever into perpetuity.

On the other hand, you shouldn't self-publish a book as an attempt to get a traditional deal for that same book. Although there are examples of authors who have done this, it is definitely NOT the norm. Most publishers will want new material in a new series.

Publishing is no longer a one-size fits all model. There are authors who are both traditionally and independently published. There are small presses that act like co-ops. Each author is expected to contribute their skills to the collective group of projects in the publishing queue. Other companies offer paid services on an a la carte menu. You can even find presses that will purchase "print-only" rights, meaning the author will self-publish the e-book while the press publishes and markets the paperback.

For this book, we won't focus on these infinite combinations, but keep in mind that while you may pursue traditional publishing with your current work in progress, you might change your mind for the next project, or the one after that.

TO RECAP

Traditional Agented – The goal is to sign a contract with one of the major publishing houses via a literary agent. The advantages are prestige, wider book distribution, and no cash outlay. The disadvantages are difficulty, time, and lower royalties.

Traditional Boutique Press – The goal is publication by a company that absorbs production costs and knows the market. The advantages are a lower bar to entry, expert publishing help, and no cash outlay. The disadvantages are less distribution and marketing, and less prestige than with the big houses.

Independent Publishing – The author has a dual-role as both creative talent and business executive. The advantages are no barrier to entry, product control, and higher royalty rates. The disadvantages are a high learning curve, less prestige, and it requires financial investment.

Hybrid Authors – Authors who publish in a variety of ways. The advantages are the ability to reap the benefits from the different publishing paths and flexibility. The disadvantages are a high learning curve, the need for patience, perseverance, and financial investment.

Chapter Three
Assessing Your Work

Unless you're Stephen King, your first draft will not be good enough to tempt agents, editors, or readers. It's the truth. In fact, most writers go through several rounds of editing before they have something that's ready for the next step.

Unfortunately, new writers all too often can't tell if or when their work is ready for the wider world. Many think their book is perfect without ever having anyone else look at it. They haven't asked for or received unbiased constructive criticism. Worse, they may operate under the faulty idea that it's an agent's or editor's job to find the diamond of a story in the rough rock of their manuscript, and then transform both book and author into a glittering bestseller.

We're going to be brutally honest. Agents, acquisition editors, and quality independent editors don't want to sort out your mess. You must have a certain level of competence before you'll get their attention. The last thing you want to do is send out a book filled with typos, plot holes, continuity errors, and grammar mistakes. Not only does it make your book look unprofessional, it wastes the readers' valuable time.

On the other side of things, some writers will spend years

and years editing and re-editing their work, thinking it's not good enough. Sometimes perfection is the enemy of good . . . or finished.

So how do you know if your work is ready to pitch or publish? Before we go any further, let's talk about the four stages of competence.

THE FOUR STAGES OF COMPETENCE

According to Noel Burch,[1] a psychologist who studied how people learn new skills, there are four stages of competence: unconscious incompetence, conscious incompetence, conscious competence, and unconscious competence.

The first is **unconscious incompetence**. In this phase, new writers don't know their work is a mess. They believe they've just written the next Great American Novel, or at least a bestseller. They think—even though it's their first finished manuscript—that the book will immediately be snatched up by an agent or editor for a large advance.

The problem is that when you're this new to the craft and the industry, you're so incompetent, you don't even know you are! This happened to Greta when she sent her first manuscript off to an editor. The woman charged $500 for a copyedit, then informed Greta that her book was boring. She was right. Greta should have sent the book to beta readers first (more on that later in this chapter) or asked for a sample edit to confirm that it was ready (which we'll discuss in Chapter Five).

Don't get discouraged. In fact, unconscious incompetence is by far the most fun stage until you arrive at mastery. Your creativity is unfettered. You don't have an inner editor to shut down, and the words often feel like they're flowing through you like water through a sieve. But at some point if you're showing your work to others, this happy bubble is going to burst.

This is good. This is growth. This is the first step toward Mastery. It's time to buckle down and learn.

Regardless of how your bubble gets burst, when it does you'll find yourself in the next stage, which is **conscious incompetence**. This painful phase is exactly what it sounds like. It's when you realize just how much you have to learn.

Many would-be writers quit at this point because they've believed the myth that either you are born with talent, or you're not. Now, while some things come more easily for some people than others, it's also not the be-all-end-all. We've all heard stories about the child with health issues who was told they'd never walk again but grew up to become an Olympic athlete. Or the child who was a terrible student only to become Einstein. Many people have progressed past their genetics to accomplish amazing things.

Whether or not you were born with a literary ear, if you want to progress as a writer, you're going to have to learn the mechanics and that just takes time, input, and practice. We all go through the phase where we realize we have a lot to learn. We need to read, take courses, write a lot of different things and one day, without realizing it, we've grown into the next stage.

Conscious competence is the stage in which you become publishable. You've got the basics down, and you've got your ego in check. Your writing isn't perfect, but you're willing to ask for constructive criticism and learn from that feedback. You'll do whatever it takes to make your book as good as it can be.

Congratulations, you're now ready to send your manuscript to professionals. If you keep on writing with this attitude, continue learning and growing, then one day you'll find you've entered the next phase: Mastery.

Unconscious competence, or mastery, is a stage many long-term writers pop in and out of. It's what we refer to as "the flow." It's that lovely place where stories seem to arrive fully formed in your mind, and you feel more like a translator than a creator.

For fiction writers, story structure, good dialogue technique, strong characterization and language use have melded into instinct within you. For nonfiction writers, you can see the organizational path your book should take from the onset. And you've found your voice. Both fiction and nonfiction writers will find they can write without constantly editing themselves. This doesn't mean they won't need to revise, or that they won't need an editor. It means they've mastered the craft.

We all go through these stages of competence with any new skill we try to learn. We may regress a level, then bounce back even better than before. We may focus on one particular aspect of our writing, like dialogue or pacing, and work through the stages just for that skill. Then do it all over again for something else.

It's like saying when you learn to walk you're going to fall down a lot. This is true, but it shouldn't discourage anyone from walking. It's just the process.

The point of all this is, although writing is a solitary process, getting good at it and getting published takes a team. It takes constructive criticism and honest feedback. A critique group is a great place to start.

CRITIQUE GROUPS

Critique groups are groups of three or more writers that meet either in person or online and agree to read one another's work for the purpose of offering constructive feedback. Like anything else in this process, a good critique group is worth its weight in gold. A bad one is writing death.

In an ideal world, you want to find a diverse group of writers from whom you can learn, but who can also learn from you. If possible, there should be members who are a few steps ahead of you in the writing game. When you want to get better at something, the best thing you can do is to spend time with people who are already where you want to be. Similarly, it's great to have published authors in the mix, because they understand what it takes to make a book salable and have already been through the publishing experience.

It's also a good idea to have members at your same level, or even a little less experienced. You'll probably be less intimidated sharing your work with them and more willing to take part in the discussion.

Now, in the above definition of a critique group, you might have noticed the words 'constructive feedback.' In order for a critique group to help you improve your writing, they absolutely *must* give criticism. It's the whole point.

That said, it's not always easy to hear that your characters behave like cardboard cutouts and your extensive world-building has slowed your story to a snail's pace. It's downright heartbreaking. But you cannot improve without first knowing what you need to improve on.

Unfortunately, some critique groups take the criticism idea a little too far. If the group is mocking or demeaning, pick up your note-book and leave. Personal attacks and intentionally nasty comments are unnecessary and only discourage your efforts. Don't let them. Pay attention to the spirit in which they offer the critique and find a group that will offer positive feedback and encouragement alongside the helpful criticism.

On the flip side, some critique groups turn into mutual admiration societies whose work nobody outside the group enjoys. This is a more common occurrence if you've skipped the first requirement: a diverse experience level. If everyone is a beginner, they might not know how to be critical. Alternatively, if everyone is too worried about hurting your feelings to tell you what's wrong, you may get a false sense that your work is ready when it's not.

Remember, agents and editors won't worry about hurting

your feelings or boosting your ego. They're only interested in buying your book if they think they can sell it to readers, so it has to be the best it can be. And readers have no fear of leaving harsh one star reviews. Don't serve yourself up for that kind of painful rejection. Find a critique group that will make your work better and prepare you and your writing for the market.

How to Find a Critique Group

There are several great ways to find a good critique group. All of them come down to networking and putting yourself out there in the writing community, either in-person or online.

One of the best ways to find a quality critique group is to join a local writing association and ask around. Most will have a critique group within their organization, sometimes a few different ones based on genre or skill level. Sometimes you have to apply to critique groups, sometimes they're open to everyone. It might take a little time and research, but with these organizational groups you'll have a better idea of the quality of the writers taking part.

If you can't find a local writing association to join or can't afford the annual membership fee, your next best bet may be the local public library. Many of them have programs specifically for writers, including lectures, and workshops, and critique groups. If they don't have one, they might help you get one started. Often, it's not for lack of interest but only lack of volunteer organizers that prevents them from building a strong writing community.

Regularly scheduled in-person meetings may not be workable for some. Maybe it's because you have a full-time day job or other full-time responsibilities that require long hours, or you may live in a rural community where a group would be too far to travel to, or maybe you just don't feel comfortable reading aloud or sharing your work in-person. If that's the case, don't despair.

There are a ton of Facebook Groups for writers of every genre and experience level. Join a few and start taking part. Some will already have established critique groups, others won't. However, Facebook Groups can be a great place to find other writers with similar books or writing styles who would be interested in starting one online.

If nothing else works, you can always try Googling "Writers' Critique Groups." You may find an online source there that works better for your lifestyle.

The Critique Partner— A More Intimate Writing Group

When Megan first started writing, she was working a full-time corporate job with a long commute. She didn't have the time or energy to take part in a weekly critique group with multiple authors. After about two years of work, she had a manuscript she thought might be good enough to publish.

However, no one else had read it, and as good as she felt about it, she knew it wasn't good enough. She needed someone to help her see the problems that she couldn't see herself, find the weaknesses in structure and dialogue, setting and pace. As a new writer, she couldn't afford a developmental editor, so she had to get creative.

In those early days, she hadn't yet connected to the writing community. She hadn't begun the journey of networking with other authors and developing friendships in the indie fantasy world. In fact, she found it difficult to admit she was a writer! (Remember, she used to work in the corporate world, where it was cool to be an analyst, but if you said you were doing something creative, eyes would glaze over and people would question your sanity.)

It turned out she knew more writers than she realized. A good friend had been a screenwriter in a prior career. Her sister, who also wrote screenplays, was working on a fantasy novel. The friend put Megan and her sister in touch, and pretty soon they were meeting every month, swapping chapters, and slowly but surely improving their craft. It took nine months, but when it was all done, Megan was confident in the story's quality and ready to show the book to the wider world.

Here's the rub, you must find someone who's able and willing to point out the flaws in your story, but who's also kind. That's why it was brilliant that Megan's critique partner was the sister of a friend. They weren't close enough to be fearful of giving real constructive criticism, but because they still had a personal relationship in common, their comments were professional and courteous.

Dedicated critique partners who mesh with your personality, goals, and writing style are difficult to find. In retrospect, Megan was lucky that she found someone so quickly. For most people, it's probably much easier to join writers' groups or search online for a critique group first, and then see if someone else in the group would be a compatible partner and interested in trading chapters or manuscripts. It's worth the effort to search for that perfect person.

Once you've gone through the critique process, it's time for the next phase of the quality control program—beta readers.

BETA READERS

Believe it or not, the term "beta reader" comes from the technology world. A "beta release" is an early prototype of a piece of software offered to the end consumer so they can test it for problems or bugs in the system. Often "beta users" get to try the software for free or at an extremely low cost for their feedback. The developers use that feedback to make improvements.

Beta readers perform the same basic task, but for books. They're individuals—often other writers or fans—who will read the first or second draft and give you critical feedback on the story. Sometimes they do it in exchange for your critique on their work, sometimes it's just because they love you and your stories.

You might think this sounds an awful lot like a critique group, and there are some similarities. The major difference between the two is that these individuals agree to read the entire manuscript from cover to cover, not just a chapter or a scene. You'll want to send them a high-quality book that's as good as you can make it on your own. You will also want to find some readers who are NOT writers, but are fans of your genre, to tell you if your book captures their interest and meets their expectations.

What aren't beta readers? People who want to boost your ego. Your mom is probably not a wonderful choice. You must find beta readers who won't hold back, who have no fear of hurting your feelings or making you angry, especially if you're not planning to hire a developmental editor.

Keep in mind, beta readers are generously giving you a significant amount of their time and energy. Respect that effort. Send them the best manuscript you can so they can give you the best, most relevant feedback possible.

How and Where to Find Beta Readers

If you're new to the writing world, you might struggle to think of people you know who are qualified to read and provide feedback on your story. This can be a significant issue if you don't already have a writer network, so make sure you go back and read the section on critique groups. Think about joining a writing group or association and taking part either in person or online.

Once you're in a group, all you really have to do is ask. Some writers will say no because they're too busy. But many writers will be more than happy to give your story a quick read and send you their notes. Even if they're not able to be a beta reader for you, they may know others who would be. Some more experienced writers may have their own beta readers they'd be willing to introduce you to. Others will know of places you can find people. Don't be pushy, but in this case, asking never hurts.

Another great place to build your author network and find potential beta readers is a writers' conference. There are hundreds of these conferences all around the country and the world, all geared toward helping writers improve their craft, find agents or editors, and grow their writing careers. Surrounding yourself with fellow wordsmiths for a week or a weekend can be incredibly inspiring, and it's an instant way to expand your connections.

Over time, as your network and your business grow, you'll develop a fan base for your stories. Maybe you write a blog or, if you're a calling-card writer, you may already have a news-letter set up to collect the email addresses of people interested in your work. (We'll talk more about newsletters in Chapter Eight.) If this is the case, definitely tap into that group of people to find qualified beta readers. They may feel incredibly honored that you would trust their opinion.

Beta Reader Selection Criteria

Different authors will look for different things when choosing beta readers. When they have them, they'll manage the process in different ways. Some send their manuscripts to only a few trusted individuals, while others will reach out to lists of fifty or more fans. Ultimately, you must figure out what works best for you and your writing process.

For example, Megan prefers five to six people in each beta reading group, and typically runs two separate beta reader groups with different goals at different points in the editing process. This gives her enough voices to gain a consensus on the aspects that still need work but doesn't overwhelm her with opinions. Greta uses two to four authors from her critique group who will read the entire manuscript.

If you're using a larger group, it's a good idea to find a diverse group of people that can provide unique perspectives into your work. You might stick to beta readers who prefer your genre, but consider including both men and women of different ethnicities, religions, nationalities, and sensitivities to help ensure the books feel well-rounded.

It's also important to make sure you're reaching the right audience for your work. For example, Mystery and Thriller readers are looking for certain key tropes and concepts. Science Fiction and Fantasy fans are interested in other things. If you're writing Women's Fiction, it's probably safe to only have female readers. Similarly, YA readers will prefer a different voice than that used in mass market adult fiction. Understanding your audience will help you dial into those preferences. There will be more on identifying your target audience in Chapter Six.

Another good subsection of individuals to include in your beta reading group—no matter the size—are subject matter experts. For example, Megan has a very important scene in *Forged in Shadow,* in which the principal character and his family forge a sword. Unfortunately, Megan doesn't have any experience working with metal. So she Googled local black-smiths and reached out to one of them to get feedback on the book. The blacksmith helped clarify the forging process and corrected some mistakes Megan had made in the descriptions.

Similarly, Megan's dad was in the Navy and is a history buff, so he reads the early drafts of her books to make sure the military aspects are believable. If you don't know an expert, Google and ask. Most of the time, it thrills people to help a writer make their books better. And who knows, you may end up with a fan.

The last type of beta reader that you might include in your group is the sensitivity reader. This is someone who will provide specific guidance on your book around issues of race, culture, sexual orientation, or other "trigger" issues. Basically, if you are writing a character in a culture or community that you are not personally a part of, a sensitivity reader will help make sure that character is three-dimensional and does not fall into stereotypes or biases. These readers have become more common in recent years, so if you're writing something that may be unintentionally controversial, you might explore this option.

Once you've selected your beta reader team, it's time to give them a focus and get the book in their hands.

How to Guide Beta Reader Feedback

Unless your beta readers are all writers, many will not know how to provide constructive criticism to help you improve your work. That's why it can be a good idea to give them a focus or a goal for their reading. There are a few different ways of doing this.

Because she uses more beta readers than Greta, Megan likes to create two groups of readers. The first group reads the book for high-level story issues, like structure, plot holes, character development, and pacing. This step comes early in her process, while she can still make large-scale changes to the story.

The second group reads the story for more technical problems, like typos and grammar issues. They'll read the book much closer to publication to help with the final proofing.

In both cases, Megan tells them up front what she's hoping to gain from their reading. She also provides an optional questionnaire to help them think about the story in alternative ways. This assists her in finding plot and character problems. You're looking for criticism that will improve the story, not just "It was great!" or "It was terrible." Generalities aren't helpful.

The questionnaire asks things like: When did you first stop reading and why? Did you connect with the characters? Were you satisfied with the climax and conclusion? It does not require readers to answer every question, only the ones that resonate or feel relevant to them. The goal is to get them mulling over the story, not to lead them toward a specific response. You can download the free template version of Megan's questionnaire in the Pro-Author Packet at www.AuthorWheel.com/ProAuthor.

That said, some readers will feel like the questionnaire is burdensome, and some writers prefer to let their beta readers have complete freedom in their responses. Greta doesn't use this—or any—questionnaire because she limits her beta readers to a few other trusted writers. They already know how to read critically. So how you manage your beta reader process is entirely up to you.

TECHNICAL CONSIDERATIONS

If you've never sent your manuscript to readers before, you may be unsure how to manage the technical aspects of distributing the book safely. You may worry about copyright infringement or pirating. Maybe the thought of managing all the comments and feedback has you feeling overwhelmed. Here are a few tips, tricks, and services you can try to ease the process.

First off, you do not have to copyright your book or mark the unpublished manuscript with that little 'c.' As the creator, you have the copyright from the moment you put word to page unless you're quoting or otherwise using someone else's words. Then you must cite sources and/or seek permission to use their content. If you're unsure about copyright laws, you can study up on them. But let's assume you're sending original material.

When sending your book to agents or editors, don't put the copyright information on the manuscript, and don't ask them to sign a non-disclosure agreement or other anti-copyright document. That's a clear indicator you're a novice writer.

Neither agents nor editors will steal your work. They generally aren't authors, and it would be bad for business even if they were.

Similarly, when you're sending the manuscript to beta readers or other critique partners, you do not need to declare your copyright. However, it may make sense to remind the readers in the email or description that the version of the book they're reading is an early draft and not for distribution. Sometimes readers get excited and want to share before the book is ready. Large publishing houses send pre-published books with the words "Advanced Reader Copy" printed on the front cover.

Another way to help keep your book from being copied or stolen is to not send a Word Doc. Instead, send an e-reader file. It won't prevent intentional theft, but it makes it more difficult for a reader to share your work accidentally. There are a few services you might use to increase the ease and security of your beta reader process.

If you don't want to send a Word doc, **Vellum** is a software that will easily create beautiful, professional e-book and PDF formats. Of course, it's possible to create the PDF directly from Word, but the benefit of Vellum is that the result will look like a book, and not a really long document. This will make the reading experience easier and more enjoyable for your beta readers and perhaps, less distracting. Plus, with Vellum you'll have all the files you need to upload to either of the next two services.

BookFunnel and **Story Origin** are sites that will take your book files and distribute them to readers for you. They offer an array of services, including promotions and landing pages, but for this discussion we'll focus on their capabilities regarding beta readers.

Both companies offer easy management and tracking of beta reader downloads, plus security benefits with unique watermarks and download links for each reader. This allows you as the author to see who's downloaded your book and is hopefully reading the story. Plus, if you discover someone has pirated your work before publication, you'll be able to track that person down.

You can set up a basic account for free and look around the sites, but ultimately you only need to choose one of them to send out your book.

Once your readers have received and read your book, it's time to track feedback. You can do this manually by asking the readers to send you their responses in an email. If you're using a reader questionnaire, you may find it easier to create a **Google Form** to track responses. Google forms collate each reader's answers into a single spreadsheet that you can review. This makes everything organized and easy to analyze, especially if you have multiple readers and want to compare their thoughts.

You can use a Google Doc to track changes and comments, or track changes in Word. There are authors who do this, Greta being one of them. Depending on which stage of editing you're in, and how well you trust your readers, it can be a good option.

Tracking changes or allowing direct comments can point out the specific typos or sections a reader had problems with. However, it can also get overwhelming if you have more than a few people providing feedback. It's also more difficult to compare responses when switching back and forth between documents. If you share a single document with multiple readers, then you open things up for discussion between them which could foster "group think."

All this may sound complicated, and perhaps it is, but that complexity gives writers more opportunity for feedback and improvement. Megan has created a system to handle it because she is an independent author. Although she hires an editor, she doesn't have access to the variety of experts a publishing house would use to get the book ready for a paying audience. She needs more help and a broader range of perspectives to ensure the book is marketable.

However, with a publishing contract and an editing team, Greta doesn't use as many beta readers. She prefers one or two trusted voices from her critique group to read her entire manuscript. As a result, she doesn't need to provide as much guidance to her beta readers. Her process is much simpler—send out the Word doc and wait for feedback.

You'll need to customize your beta reader process for your needs and goals.

TO RECAP

There are **four stages of competence** that we must all work through in order to master a skill:

- Unconscious incompetence
- Conscious incompetence
- Conscious competence
- Unconscious competence

Critique groups are groups of three or more writers that meet either in person or online and agree to read one another's work for the purpose of offering constructive feedback. You can find critique groups in writers' groups or associations, in Facebook groups, or by Googling them online.

Beta Readers are individuals who will read your entire first or second draft to give you critical feedback on the story. When choosing your group of beta readers, consider:

- Group size
- Diversity
- Target audience
- Experts
- Sensitivity readers

When considering **how to send your work to readers**, look into these services:

- Vellum for formatting
- BookFunnel or StoryOrigin for distribution
- Google Forms for collecting and collating reader responses
- Beta Reader Questionnaire – A sample questionnaire is included in the appendix of this book.

Chapter Four
The Steps to a Traditional Deal

After reading Chapter Three, you may have discovered your work isn't ready to send to editors or agents yet. That's okay, there's still plenty to do on the business side of things before you pitch or contact independent editors. The writing life is one of constant learning and developing. Keep on honing your craft and revising your manuscript. You can prepare to approach the pros at the same time.

Before we talk about how to query agents and acquisition editors, let's go over the differences between them. You'll approach them both the same way, but it's good to understand the role each plays in the publishing industry.

AGENTS AND ACQUISITION EDITORS

A literary agent's job is to identify, pitch, and ultimately broker a publishing contract for the authors and manuscripts they represent. They do this in exchange for a percentage of any advance and royalties made when that work is published.

Never work with an agent who wants to charge you up front. A genuine agent is in a commission sales position. If they can't sell your book to a publisher, they won't make money. If they sell it, but the publisher doesn't market it well, they won't make money. It's the risk they take on when they sign up for the job.

This is why agents are so difficult to get. They can't afford to spend time on a book they don't believe will sell well. However, once you find one that believes in your work, they can be valuable players to have on your side. As mentioned in Chapter Two, they have expertise and industry connections you don't have, and they can shape a career and help you find your way as an author.

It can be a good idea for all aspiring authors, whatever path they choose for publication, to have a literary agent review their work. They understand the market probably better than any other industry professional and can tell you whether your book is truly ready to pitch or publish. It never hurts to have a fresh set of eyes read your story.

Keep in mind, if you're turned down by an agent, it doesn't mean they think your work stinks. It may mean they've recently taken on a similar project, or it may mean they don't have the right connections to sell it. The publishing industry is massive, so make sure you're asking the right questions of an agent who represents your genre and has sold books similar to your own.

Often agents only represent certain types of books. Some agents only work with nonfiction authors, others with literary authors, others love genre fiction. Part of your homework will be to find a suitable match for your manuscript.

Having said all that, a bad agent is worse than no agent. They can stall a career. It can take an excellent agent a year, or even longer, to sell your book. A bad agent may never try, or may promote your story to the wrong market. Two years later you have no publishing deal and no agent, and you're back to square one.

Acquisition editors, on the other hand, work for only one publisher. They take submissions from agents (or sometimes directly from authors if they accept unsolicited or unagented manuscripts) and decide which books their press would like to publish. When they like a book, they will invest in it, first by offering the author a publishing contract and often an "advance"—an upfront payment to the author against future royalties.

Unlike the agent, the acquisition editor's paycheck is not dependent on your book sales. However, publishers sign things they believe will make money, and it's an acquisition editor's job to know what they're looking for.

Remember: a small press should do essentially all the same things a larger press will do for you. Just like the big publishing houses, they will have an acquisitions editor who will decide which books to offer contracts. However, some of them will be open to submissions from authors who don't have agents, especially when the press is new. Go back to Chapter Two for the complete discussion on the difference between Traditional Agented and Traditional Boutique publishing.

FINDING YOUR PERFECT MATCH

An agent Greta met at a conference a few years back told her she received on average a thousand submissions a month. Out of that number, she only took on about five books. Attempting to get a deal with an agent or a small press without an introduction is a bit like winning the lottery. Some people do it, but it's better to hedge your bets.

Ask anyone in sales—a warm lead beats a cold one any day of the week. If an agent or acquisition editor can put a face to a query letter, he or she is much more likely to read it. In this first stage of the game, that's your goal. Later we'll worry about fine-tuning your sales pitch, but for now, you just want to make some contacts.

An introduction from another author will almost always get you an audience, however it's not polite to ask for a referral to their agent or publishing house. If they offer, that's great, but don't take offense if they don't. The bottom line is, if you want a traditional deal, you're going to have to do some research.

One thing to keep in mind is that this is a two-way street. You are the talent. After all, if writers didn't write, publishers wouldn't have a product to publish. Just because an agent or acquisition editor says she represents the kind of book you've written doesn't mean you want to work with her.

Before Greta signed with her current publisher, another boutique press offered her a contract. She popped the champagne cork, did a jig, and rejoiced. The next day, she checked them out. Their website and their Facebook page set off alarm bells. She didn't like their book covers. There were typos in their website copy. Their books had few, or poor, Amazon reviews.

She decided to do a bit of investigative work. She sent a friend request to one of their authors on Facebook. This author had books published with a variety of publishers. When she accepted Greta's request, Greta sent a message and asked about her experience with this particular boutique press. The author said she did one book with them and that was enough for her. Greta turned down that contract.

Because the query process is so difficult and writers receive so many rejections, the temptation is to jump at the first "yes" that comes. But just as a bad agent is worse than no agent, a bad publisher is worse than no publisher.

Once you sign that contract, your story is in their hands. If they hire a poor editor, slap on an unprofessional cover, and never do more than tweet about your book launch, it reflects on you. Most readers don't care who publishes a book. They don't even notice. But your name is in bold letters on the front cover.

Try approaching the pursuit of a deal the way you might approach house hunting. Sit down and make lists.

First, write down the things you have to have, the

non-negotiables. For Greta, this included print and digital books. She wanted to see her work in bookstores. Small independent stores were fine, but the publisher had to have bookstore connections. Their books must be well edited and have professional covers. The author stable must be one she'd be happy to be part of. Their books must have more reviews than she could get on her own.

Next, write down the things you hope for, but aren't deal breakers. For her, this list included a marketing manager and some input in cover design and book pricing.

Finally, make your this-would-be-amazing list. Greta wanted a company that would attempt to sell subsidiary rights and enter her titles in book award contests. She got everything she'd hoped for when she signed with her publisher, including her this-would-be-amazing list. So can you, but it will take research and patience.

Sometimes you'll need to stalk the agent or publisher of your dreams on social media to find out what they're all about, and where you could meet them. You could also look for writing events hosting industry professionals you might be interested in working with.

Many writers' conferences have early submission options, where you pay an additional fee to submit part of your manuscript (usually the first ten to fifteen pages) for review and critique by an agent or editor of your choice. That you are willing to invest in your work is a sign to them that you are taking this whole writing thing seriously, which makes them take you more seriously. There are also meet and greet events, generally in the bar, and some agents and editors will attend "read and critiques" to listen to the work being workshopped. We have several friends who have found their agents through local conferences.

Another way to get personal attention from agents and editors is to submit your work to writing contests, or award competitions. These are typically online events and some offer representation by an agent, or a manuscript read-through from a publisher as a prize. Even if that isn't what's offered, winning a prize looks great in a query letter. Writers' Digest and other writers' magazines and associations often have lists of these contests and their deadlines.

Another type of online contest becoming more mainstream is the Twitter pitch. Here's how they work: Someone, usually another author, contacts a list of editors and agents and asks them if they'll agree to check a certain hashtag on a certain day during certain hours. Writers tweet their book descriptions using the event hashtag. The industry professionals then hit the "like" button on your tweet if they want you to send them a full query.

Each contest has its own rules about how many tweets you can send and when you can send them, but most recommend you change your pitch each time. This gives you a chance to see which bait attracts the most fish and helps you write the logline for your query letter. (We'll go in depth on how to write a logline in Chapter Six.) A logline is an essential ingredient in any query or book proposal and later can be used to market your published book.

Finally, there are also websites where you can find agents and editors who are looking for authors. These professionals are often deluged with pitches after they're listed on the sites, so it's not exactly a warm lead, but at least you can mention where you saw them. It shows you're doing your homework.

GETTING READY TO PITCH

So now that you know where to meet agents and editors, what happens when you do? Like anything else in life, there is a protocol. You want to put your best foot forward and that means looking and sounding like a professional and presenting a professional product.

The first time Greta met with an agent, she had no idea what she was doing. She'd sent an early submission into the Southern California Writers' Conference in Irvine. She paid fifty dollars, sent ten pages of her manuscript to an agent who was planning to attend, and received a fifteen-minute appointment.

Prior to writing fiction, her background was nonfiction: a self-help book, magazine articles, and marketing copy. In all those disciplines, edgy and unique ways of expressing concepts are not only accepted, they're expected. This is her way of explaining why she thought describing her novel as "cozy horror" was a good idea. It wasn't.

The agent pointed out, very kindly, that while she could call her genre anything she wanted on her own website, there were certain industry standards and "cozy horror" wasn't one of them. The agent said Greta's book was a thriller with supernatural elements.

You can avoid a similar embarrassing moment by knowing where your manuscript fits on the bookstore shelf, be it digital or physical. There are several reasons this is important. Knowing the genre will give agents and editors instant insight into the story. They are busy people. They don't have time to listen to you explain the plot of your sci-fi-romance-thriller-western, especially if that's not a genre they specialize in.

Similarly, knowing your genre is essential for targeting readers. Different genres have different 'rules.' Romance readers want a happily-ever-after ending and multiple points of view. Thriller readers want a fast-paced plot with high stakes. Mystery and suspense readers want twists and turns. Knowing your genre will help you write a better book, one that meets those reader expectations.

Once you know your genre, and know the kind of reader you're targeting, it becomes much easier to find beta readers for the editing stages and market the book after publication.

If you're writing nonfiction, understanding your genre is a

bit easier. Calling-card writers' books fit into the category of their business or service. If you're writing a memoir, well, your category is memoir. Fiction writers are the ones who most often get snagged on this issue.

New fiction writers often don't understand the nuances of their chosen genre. When you ask them what they're writing, they launch into a long description of the plot of their story. Most people only want to hear the genre and logline.

You probably have some idea of what you're writing. You know if it's mystery and thriller, science fiction and fantasy, romance, or general fiction. If these definitions are new to you, we suggest you do an internet search and read up on the basics before you dive into the project below.

However, even if you know the broad genre category, you might not have stopped to analyze the sub-genre. For instance, you know your book is a thriller, but don't know whether it's geo-political, psychological, or a police procedural.

The following exercise is good for all writers who desire to eventually sell their stories to agents, editors, or readers.

Genre Exercise Step 1: Research Other Titles

Do an online search to find books similar to yours and make a list of the bestsellers or the ones that have won awards in the past two or three years. Take that list and a legal pad and head to your local library. If you don't have access to a library, use Amazon as your virtual library by reading the samples and copyright pages for each title.

Find as many of those titles as you can and bring them to a table (real or virtual.) Then take notes.

Genre Exercise Step 2: Take Notes on the Following

- Titles – What are the similarities in length, wording, or themes? We all remember the "Girl" titles of a few years back. Often, you'll see a trend.

- Length – How many pages do they have? How many chapters? Are the chapters long or short or of varied lengths? This is a bit more difficult to assess on Amazon unless you buy the books, but you can at least see the first chapter. However, it's not a bad idea to read the bestsellers in your genre. Writers need to read.
- Point of View – Is it in first person? Third person close or distant? How many POV (point of view) characters does it have?
- Style – Look at the length of the sentences. Is the language casual or formal? How much white space is on the page? How much description? How much dialogue?
- Plot – What are the common themes? Read the book synopsis on the back covers or the sales pages. Note where the stories intersect.
- Opening Hook – Read the first pages. How does the author hook the reader? This is more important than we have time to discuss here, but there are many courses and books dedicated to hooking your reader in the first sentence, page, and chapter. In fact, at Author Wheel, we teach an entire workshop called "First Page, Lasting Impression" and offer a first page critique service.

Is the book a standalone novel, or is it part of a series? We'll have more about writing a series in Chapter Eight, but it's good to see what others are doing.

You can use this information to polish your manuscript and present it to agents or editors. The more you know about what's selling in your genre, the more professional you will sound. The more professional you sound, the better chance you have of attracting attention in a noisy world.

Once you know your genre and subgenre, and have done your market research, it's time to write your query letter. A query letter is like a résumé for a fiction book. A book proposal has the same function for a nonfiction book. There are things that should be included and things that shouldn't, and they each have a unique format. Writing a query or book proposal is an art unto itself.

While you're researching your dream team, or waiting for the next conference or Twitter pitch, get started on your query letter or book proposal. This isn't a quick email that you simply sit down and send out: They're almost as difficult to write as your book was. Some authors find them *more* difficult.

However, once you've met with a professional and gotten that warm lead, you're going to want to act fast. Agents and editors receive so many submissions, they will forget all about you if you dawdle around for weeks with your letter. You need to have it ready to go.

There are many websites and online courses focused solely on how to write a good query letter or book proposal. There are also people you can hire to write it for you. We've included a few of these resources in the appendix of this book, but here are the basics.

ANATOMY OF A QUERY LETTER

The first and perhaps most important thing to consider is the person you're sending your letter to. Tailor your letter to the guidelines on their website. Not all agents or publishers ask for the same thing. This goes back to respect. Don't waste their time. Stand out in a good way. Show them that if they choose to work with you, you can follow instructions and do what's asked of you.

When it comes to the introduction in your query, remember nobody wants a form letter, including you. Let this person know you've taken the time to research them, or remind them you met them somewhere, or that they responded to your Twitter pitch. Anything you can do to keep your query out of the slush pile, to make your letter read like a human being wrote it, is going to help.

Next, you want to give them the gist of your pitch in one sentence. Mention the length, genre, and comparison authors. An example would be: My 80,000 word Women's Fiction novel will be enjoyed by readers who love Ellen Hilderbrand's relatable characters and Jan Karen's warmth and small town setting. You've told them a lot in one sentence.

Then you'll want to give them the logline you've written and tested—more on this in Chapter Six. This will introduce your synopsis.

One mistake writers make when writing their synopsis is thinking it's the same thing as the plot. Yes, you must say what happens, but all plots have been written. There is nothing new under the sun. Focus on what makes your story different from the rest. We go into much more detail on this in Chapter Six as well.

The biography section follows the synopsis. Remember, a query letter isn't a job application. The agent or publisher wants to know what qualifies you to write this book. If you're a published writer, tell them. If your story features a veterinarian who solves murders and you're a vet, tell them. If you're an accountant and your story has nothing to do with finances, don't tell them.

Most agents and editors will ask for sample pages. Generally, they'll want those pages pasted into the email or a specific place on a submission form, not as an attachment or a PDF. The exception to this is when they've had contact with you and know you're not a troll sending them malware. Even then, don't send attachments unless they've specifically asked for them. The wild-west internet has created problems for many.

Finally, be professional. But not too professional unless you're targeting professionals. In other words, try to use the tone, or voice, you use in your manuscript. If your book is funny, it's okay to use a little humor in the letter. If it's literary, you can be literary in the synopsis.

But don't be weird. Don't be too familiar, or too humorous. We know this sounds like common sense, but we've heard horror stories about women sending naked photos to male agents hoping they'll pick up their story for 'special favors' and editors being followed into public restrooms and being pitched while they urinated. Seriously. Don't be weird.

THE NONFICTION BOOK PROPOSAL

Much of what was just said about writing a fiction query letter also applies to a nonfiction book proposal. The best line of defense with a book proposal is the same as it is with a fiction query: follow the instructions on the agent or publisher's website.

The major difference between a query and a book proposal is in the synopsis. Rather than write a plot summary, you'll include an outline of your chapter headings and a good description of the content of your book.

The biography section is more important for the nonfiction book proposal. They'll want to know your expertise and qualifications regarding the topic and your audience reach. If you already have a business around your topic, they'll want to know that. If you have a newsletter or existing audience, they'll want to know that, too. You may also have to submit a marketing blueprint, identifying your target market and how you intend to reach them.

Unlike with fiction, your manuscript rarely needs to be complete, but you may have to include—or they may later request—a sample chapter or two to prove your writing skill. Make sure you have something ready to go.

Once you know your genre and have written your query letter or book proposal, there's one more thing to do before you pitch.

TRACKING SUBMISSIONS AND DEALING WITH REJECTION

When a writer begins the query process, they will be rejected—not maybe, possibly, or sometimes. It's a universal experience. Unless your father owns a publishing company or your mother is a celebrity, it's a safe bet when you shop your manuscript around, you're going to hear the big N-O more than once.

Rejection teaches you a lot about the industry. You'll meet successful agents you'd never be able to work with, even if they wanted to sign you. You'll investigate reputable publishing houses where you'd be miserable. The query process will help you fine-tune your wish list.

Before you send your first query letter or book proposal, make a spreadsheet that includes columns for name, company, date you pitched, what you sent, date you can expect a response, and the response. You will forget who you sent what to if you don't.

Also, include a section for notes. This is where you can jot down what they said, where you met them or heard about them, and so on. If you're not good with spreadsheets, never fear. We've included a link to a pre-made spreadsheet for you in the appendix.

The notes section is especially important for grading your rejections. Before Greta signed with a publisher, she pitched around seventy-five agents and editors. That may sound like a lot, but it's not that many in the grand scheme of things. It can be a painful process, but it's always an education.

If every rejection throws you into despair, you'll never find success. Too many writers give up on the query process and either self-publish (not as an author-entrepreneur, which is a serious and professional undertaking, but alone, without resources, and desperate) or walk away. Make it your mission to learn from every rejection.

Greta got to the point where she graded them. Bad rejections were form letters and silences. Better rejection letters were personal. The best rejections told her what was wrong with the work so she could improve.

When you receive a form letter, it means the person you pitched was so disinterested, or busy, or overwhelmed, he or she didn't read it thoroughly. Form letters, or silences, mean you pitched the wrong person, it was bad timing, your query letter or book proposal needs help, or they weren't looking for what you wrote.

Form letters don't mean your writing is bad, your book premise is bad, or that you're an abject failure. When you're pitching, it's very important to get honest feedback on your work from other writers who are further ahead than you are, in other words, a critique group. Take your criticism from them, and don't second guess this process.

After every ten to fifteen rejections, it's a good idea to re-read your query and opening pages, or book proposal with a critical eye. Ask for input. What can you change to make it better? Tweak, revise, and resend.

At some point in this process, you'll begin to get personal rejections in which an agent or editor tells you what they liked and what they didn't like. Some of these will be painful. But they're actually a good sign. They mean you've moved up the ladder a few rungs.

Personal rejections tell you you're getting closer. You may even consider revising based on what they say. You may home in on the type of person you're pitching. You may even find your letter is the problem.

An editor from a boutique press Greta really wanted to publish with once sent her a long letter explaining why he wouldn't buy her manuscript. One of his criticisms was that her protagonist wasn't likable. All her beta readers had found her main character very likable. In fact, one critique she'd received was that the character was too nice!

Her first thought was to call that editor up and tell him

how wrong he was. Her protagonist was a doll, a gem. He'd completely misunderstood her. Then she had an epiphany. He only had the first ten pages of the manuscript and her synopsis. One or both were at fault.

The synopsis was the culprit. In her attempt to prove her character had an emotional arc, was deep and complex, Greta had exaggerated the character flaws. She rewrote the query letter and began getting requests for full manuscripts. The rejections really got interesting after that.

The last type of rejection you might receive is called a revise and resubmit request. These rejections come when an agent or editor has liked your query enough to ask for more pages— sometimes fifty, sometimes a full manuscript. It's always a nail-biting time when your work is out there in the world being read and critiqued.

If they decide not to take the book as it is, you'll receive either a personal rejection or a revise and resubmit request. If you get the second, you have a choice. Will you? Or, won't you? There are several things to consider before you revise your manuscript.

First, how much do you want to work with this agent or publishing house? Are you just feeling desperate? Or is this someone you really respect? Then, whether or not you respect them, is this person respected in the industry? Or are they as new as you are? And finally, do you agree with their assessment? Does their advice ring true?

Greta received a request to revise and resubmit before she got a contract. It was from a boutique publisher who felt her book didn't fit neatly into any one genre. The editor thought parts read like a thriller, parts like a romance, and parts were very literary. She suggested Greta make up her mind.

She was right. In fact, this was when Greta came up with the idea to go to the library and look at the books in the genre she thought she was writing in. It was a fabulous and eye-opening exercise. She rewrote the book as a suspense story. That publisher never accepted that manuscript, but Greta signed a contract for the entire *Seven Deadly Sins* series from another publisher after the rewrite.

However, we know another author whose agent had him rewrite and rewrite until there was no life left in the book, and then canceled his contract. This author went back to an earlier version of the story, got another agent and a publishing deal. That book won a local book award.

Our final word of advice is to have courage going through the pitch/rejection cycle. It can be very discouraging if you don't see it as a time of learning and growth. Thank every agent and every editor who rejects you for their time. Believe it or not, they're trying to help you. And celebrate every victory, no matter how small.

TO RECAP

Agents work with many publishing houses and only get paid when you get paid. Good places to connect with agents are at conferences, writers' events, contests, and pitch fests.

Acquisition editors work for one publishing house. If they are accepting manuscripts directly from authors, they most likely work for a small or boutique press.

Small boutique presses don't always offer advances, but generally offer a larger royalty share than the larger publishers, and you won't have to share with your agent.

Be prepared before you pitch by knowing both your genre and your subgenre. Complete the Genre Exercise to research your specific target market.

Anatomy of a Fiction Query Letter:
- Tailor your letter to the individual you're pitching.
- Say something personal in the introduction.

- Follow the guidelines on the website exactly.
- Write a good logline or hook.
- Let him or her know length, genre, and possible comparison authors.
- Write a short (three paragraph at most) synopsis.
- Write a short (one paragraph) bio of pertinent information.
- Never send an attachment unless it's specifically requested.
- Be professional.

The Nonfiction Book Proposal:

- Tailor your letter to the individual you're pitching.
- Say something personal in the introduction.
- Follow the guidelines on the website exactly.
- Write a good logline or hook.
- Let him or her know length, topic, and possible comparison authors.
- Write a chapter by chapter summary.
- Write a bio of pertinent information.
- Write a marketing proposal that includes knowledge of your target audience and how you plan to reach them.
- Never send an attachment unless it's specifically requested.
- Be professional.

Tracking Your Queries

You can download a sample spreadsheet in the Pro-Author Packet by visiting www.AuthorWheel.com/ProAuthor and joining our list.

Chapter Five
Steps to Independent (Self) Publishing

Independent publishing is all about organization and objectivity. Whereas authors pursuing traditional publication can rely on the expertise of their publisher's decisions, indies must navigate the process on their own. However, because you're not relying on decision-by-committee, you're able to move at your own pace and control every piece of the final product.

Independent publishing may be a faster path to market than the traditional path, but publishing always takes time, especially the first time. We won't lie. It's a lot of work, but so is trying to get an agent or editor. Independent publishing requires a different kind of work with different goals and different outcomes. Ultimately, some people are more suited to one publishing path than another.

Like Megan, you may have decided early on that you wanted to pursue the indie path. Or, you may have planned to seek a traditional deal, read Greta's section on that path, and are now reconsidering. Regardless, we encourage you to educate yourself on both options. If you understand the entire publishing industry, it will help you decide what's best for you and your books.

Before we get into the nitty-gritty of going indie, it's important to take a moment to complete a self-inventory.

THE INDIE SELF-INVENTORY

In the beginning of this book, we talked about your author personality and how hard it is to know where you're going if you don't know where you're starting from. You need to take an introspective look at who you are and analyze your goals, situation, and skill set before you can make an educated choice about how to shape your author career. The same is true now, only this time you'll be deciding how to shape your publishing business.

As an indie, you not only have to write a fantastic book, you also have to create a product that readers want to buy. In a word: packaging. This includes the exterior cover, the interior format, and the clarity of your words. Some of these things we can do ourselves, but some will require outside help, either from hired professionals, traded services, or even the generosity of friends.

Remember, there's a reason we prefer the term independent author to self-publishing: you can't do everything by yourself. However, you can do some things. So before you hire assistance, let's look at what you bring to the table.

What are your strengths? What skills make you an excellent candidate for independent publishing? Are you self-motivated? Do you have experience in business, marketing, or finance? Do you write cleanly with few typos or grammatical errors? Or, better yet, do you have experience as a professional editor? Are you comfortable with Photoshop?

For example, with an undergraduate business degree and seven years of experience working for a large accounting firm,

Megan knows how to handle a spreadsheet. She's not afraid of numbers. She likes them. During her time in the corporate world, she wrote reports and professional emails for clients. This taught her to write cleanly and concisely, a skill that has made her editors happy. Some have even given her a slightly cheaper rate because of it. She's also highly self-motivated and loved the idea of running her own business. The indie road was a great fit for Megan.

Once you understand your strengths, it's time to look at your weaknesses. These are always tough questions for people to answer, but it's important to be as honest as possible. Where do you think you'll need help? What skills are you lacking that are critical to bring a book to market?

Let's go back to Megan as an example. She's an introvert, even online. While she's not afraid of public speaking, put her in a room with a hundred strangers and she'll turn into a wallflower. She finds it hard to connect with new people and to promote herself and her work. She's not great at marketing. (This is why she and extroverted Greta make such a wonderful team.)

Megan also readily admits she doesn't have any skills in graphic design. She knew she'd need to hire cover designers. To this day, she often seeks help for banner images and other marketing artwork. When Megan realized where her strengths and weakness lay she was able to educate herself on her options.

When you're just starting out, you may not have the money to hire professionals to do everything you're not stellar at. Don't despair. There are many excellent software programs available to help you bring your book into the world. Consider things like Excel, Photoshop, Scrivener, Vellum, Word, InDesign, Pages, Google, Facebook, Instagram, Canva . . . The list is long and sometimes overwhelming.

Our advice is to list the programs you already use and then decide how much time you're willing to spend learning new strategies and technologies. To speed up the publishing process, you may want to consider paying someone else to do the job. If you have a lot of money and not a lot of time, hire someone. If you're short on cash, you may need to study, or trade services with someone else.

Which brings us to our last point. As with any business, you must have startup capital. How much money are you *willing* to invest in your book? What seems reasonable, given your skill set and goals?

For example, if you're a bucket-lister who only wants to publish your book to share with friends and family, a few hundred dollars may be your limit. However, if your goal is to be a career author-entrepreneur, you'll need more for professional covers, editing, and promotions.

Take your time walking through these questions. Don't rush it. This is the foundation on which you'll build your independent publishing business.

Hiring an Editor

Now that you've figured out (more or less) what you can do yourself, it's time to think about who you're going to hire and how much it's going to cost.

There is a huge and diverse list of service providers that you might bring onto your team. For the purposes of this book, we're going to focus on the three primary contractors you must hire to get your book ready for sale: Editor, Cover Designer, and Formatter. Arguably the most important of these is the editor.

As the author, your book is your baby. In your eyes, your baby is—if not perfect—certainly beautiful. You're likely so enamored with it, it's difficult to see its flaws. But unlike an actual baby, other people won't hesitate to judge it. A book is fair game for tough reviewers and critics. Since you're asking people to pay to read your work, it's only natural they'll expect value.

Traditionally published authors go through a rigorous editing process, and indies who want to be professional must mimic that. Usually this starts with critique groups and beta readers, as discussed in Chapter Three, but indies must take their manuscript to the next level or risk publishing a book filled with plot holes and errors. Even editors need copyeditors and proofreaders for their own work.

Unfortunately, editing is expensive. As an independent author, you're always looking for ways to cut costs. You might be tempted to cut this one. You may believe you're tough enough on yourself to be objective about your work. Ninety-nine percent of the time, you'll be wrong.

The brain is a magnificent liar. Studies have shown that the creator of the text will overlook errors while reading, because their brain already knows what they're trying to say. You know your story so thoroughly you physically cannot see the mistakes in the text. Your brain will fix them as you read. An external perspective is essential to ensure your message is clear, your prose is coherent, and your grammar is sound.

What many people don't realize is that there are many types of editors. In fact, within the big traditional publishing houses, most books will go through at least three, often four different editors before publication. As an indie, you won't need to hire all of them, but it's good to know what each type of editor does and how much a freelancer would cost if you used them.

Developmental Editor

A developmental editor helps shape the story. They will cost you anywhere from $500 to $3,000 or more. This person focuses mainly on plot, character, pacing, setting, and other story structure concepts. They'll be the one to tell you if a character's motivation is hollow, if you've missed a major plot point, or if your story is dragging on too long.

In the modern traditional publishing world, this kind of

editing often takes place *before a writer* gets an agent. People seeking a traditional deal sometimes hire a developmental editor after receiving several rejections. For indies, a developmental edit comes after self-editing, but before the copyeditor gets his or her hands on the manuscript.

For both traditional and independent authors, hiring a professional is the fastest way to find problems and fix the book. There are other ways to achieve a developmental edit through critique partners, critique groups, and beta readers however. Go back to Chapter Three if you need a refresher on this topic.

Copyeditor

The copyeditor reads the book for clarity and prose problems. They look for typos and grammar errors to make sure the text complies with *The Chicago Manual of Style* or another written style guide. They may also highlight inconsistencies. For example, a character who starts out with blue eyes, but later has green eyes would be flagged. Sometimes they'll catch story issues that the developmental editor didn't or that you didn't resolve well enough. A good copyeditor will run you between $500 and $2,500 or more, depending on the length of the book. At the time of this writing, the standard price for a copyedit is $0.02 per word, however different editors may charge more or less depending on their level of experience and qualifications.

Proofreader

The proofreader is the last set of eyes on the manuscript before publication. In the traditional world, they usually review a printed copy of the book to find typos and formatting errors. In the indie world, if you're doing a paperback, it helps to have someone read that version, but you can also have them read a Kindle or e-book copy. Regardless, their job is not to comment on the characters or the story, but to read each word with a critical eye. They make sure you don't spell too t-w-o instead of t-o-o.

Many copyeditors (but not all) will offer a package deal of copyediting and proofing. If you have to hire them separately, it could cost you anywhere from $500 to $1,500.

Acquisitions Editor

Another type of editor we will not get into here because indies don't have to worry about them, is the acquisitions editor. These editors read manuscripts submitted by writers or agents to a particular publishing house. Their job is to decide if the publisher should buy the rights. Sometimes, acquisitions editors also act as developmental or copyeditors for that publisher.

If you're gasping with shock right now, we understand. Editors are expensive. If you didn't know it before, now you do. But the good news is that there are ways to cut costs without losing quality.

For example, a talented group of beta readers might cancel the need for a developmental editor. If one of those readers is a typo hound, they might do a final proofing pass for you.

There are also several ways to trade or barter services to get your costs down. We have author friends who trade manuscripts and edit for one another. Others will trade different services. For example, if you are a visual artist, you could trade cover design for editing.

If you don't have the cash, go back to your Self-Inventory Worksheet and look at all the things you can offer other writers or editors. You may have to be creative, but hey, that's why they call writers "creatives."

COVER DESIGN AND FORMATTING

While your book is sitting with the editor, it's time to think about the packaging. We're not talking about shipping supplies—boxes and tape and such. We're talking about the physical design of your product. Even bucket-listers should consider how and where they want to present their book.

Every genre has format and design expectations. If you haven't done the exercise in Chapter Four about understanding your genre, do it now. You'll need a good sense of what's selling in categories similar to your book's. What do the covers look like? Who designed them? What do the interiors look like? Are these e-book-only books, or also in paperback?

Once you have this information, you can evaluate your own work. Your first critical decision is in where and how you're going to sell your book. Will you create only digital copies? Paperback? Hardback? Will you sell on Amazon Kindle exclusively, which is the easiest and fastest way to get your book "out there." Or do you want to go "wide" and sell on Barnes & Noble, Apple Books, and Kobo to name a few? There's more on this at the end of the chapter.

Each format and platform has different requirements for the books they list for sale. For example, if you're only going to sell e-books, you don't need a back cover designed for your book and the interior formatting will be relatively simple. That could save you some cash. A hardcover not only requires a back cover, it may also require a dust jacket with an inside flap on front and back, and readers will expect a fancier interior.

Don't be afraid to ask for referral or quantity discounts, either. If you refer a friend who hires them, the designer might offer a discount as a thank you. If you're writing a series and can book three covers in advance, they may be willing to give you a discount on the package deal. Similarly, you might be able to network with other authors needing covers and receive a group discount if you hire the designer together. Guaranteed work has value.

Before you hire anyone, make sure you've thought through your sales plan. Once you have one, you can start putting together your cover design and formatting.

Cover Design

One of the most enjoyable indie author tasks is choosing a cover designer and working with them to create a visual representation of your book. You may already have great ideas for what you want your cover to look like. Or, you might feel a little lost about what will sell best. Either way, a good cover designer will help bring your book to life.

You might think your marketing research has prepared you to make your own cover, that this would be a great way to save cash. Unless you're a professional graphic designer, we strongly recommend hiring a pro.

Not all covers are expensive, and an experienced designer will know the ins and outs of creating a cover that will pass the e-book and print standards of the various distributors. Ideally, they should also be skilled in your particular genre and know the design elements that draw your target market.

There are three basic choices for cover design, each with a wide range of pricing. Your choice will depend a lot on your genre and budget.

Premade Covers

Premade covers are typically created with Photoshop and stock photography, using a method called photo manipulation. These covers begin life as practice designs or portfolio builders for the artists and can cost as little as $25 or $50. When you buy a premade, the artist will customize the title for you, but otherwise it's considered a finished design, which is why they are so inexpensive.

Keep in mind, a $50 premade is only going to get you in the door. It may be absolutely gorgeous, but it wasn't created with your book in mind. Sometimes you'll get lucky and find the perfect cover to fit your content, but often they won't be exactly right. That might be okay. Your job is to draw readers in, not tell the story word for word in images. But keep in mind you only get one chance to make a first impression.

Custom Photo Manipulation Covers

If you want something specific to your book or branded for your series, that's still not crazy expensive, you'll want a custom photo manipulation cover. Depending on the designer, these can range from about $100 (typically new designers still looking to expand their portfolio and build a client base) to $1,000 (experienced, heavily booked designers who often include marketing images and other services in a package deal).

These covers are created using the same process as the premade covers. With stock photography and a skilled use of Photoshop, they can be a great value for the money. However, even though a photo manipulation cover can be customized to your book, the available stock imagery limits the design.

Many designers reuse popular stock photographs repeatedly. In fact, the model used on Megan's series, *The Sanyare Chronicles,* is now a favorite for book covers because she creates stock photo sets in different costumes and poses. This is great for series writers. When Megan commissioned the cover for *The Last Descendant,* the model was unknown. Now, if you scroll through the Amazon Kindle fantasy or science-fiction bestsellers, you'll see her on half a dozen titles. For her latest release, Megan chose a fully illustrated cover.

Fully Illustrated Covers

If, like Megan, you're concerned about having the same models or photos as other books on the market, your only choice is to commission a custom piece of art. This will be either an exclusive photoshoot or a painted illustration. It is far and away the most expensive option. It also takes the most time and requires the most guidance from the author, which is something you must factor into your timeline for publication.

Some illustrators may not be experienced with cover layout and typography design. If they are, you may get a deal by combining both the artwork and the design. However, often you must hire a second person to incorporate an illustrator's art into the final e-book and print layout.

As you might imagine, the price range of an illustrated cover is really wide. An illustrator or custom photoshoot could cost as little as $300 or as much as $1000, sometimes even more. An experienced graphic designer could add another $300 to $1000 depending on the complexity of the layout and / or customization of the typography. For Megan, it made sense to spend the extra money because illustrated covers are common, even expected, in the epic fantasy genre.

Formatting

Interior book design is cover design's less-sexy cousin, but it's still important. A good interior design should be beautiful, but it should never distract from the reading experience. The words shouldn't feel cramped on the page, however fewer pages decreases the print cost. Finding a happy medium is essential.

If you can visit your local library for your genre research, make sure you pay attention to the interior format. Look at the font size, the chapter headers, the location of page numbers and titling on each page. How wide are the margins? How much space is between each line of text? Once again, you'll want to meet your reader's expectations, and each genre will be a little different because of the target audience.

There are two different formats publishers typically produce: a print PDF for paperbacks and an ePub file for e-books. There are several ways you can create these files, from do-it-yourself, to free services, to purchased software, or you can always hire a pro.

Do-It-Yourself

The do-it-yourself method is best for writers who either already use Scrivener as their word processor of choice, have experience with InDesign, or know HTML coding. Even with experience, there will probably be a learning curve, and perhaps a few weeks and some frustration to get it right. The advantage is you'll have full control of all your files. This can be a tremendous benefit if you expect to have lots of future changes. Plus, doing it yourself is free if you already have the programs installed on your computer.

Free Conversion Services

However, if you're less particular about the design of your book and want to save the money, there are also several free services that will convert your Word file into the print and e-book formats. In fact, many of the e-book distributors—including Smashwords, Draft2Digital, and Amazon—produce excellent books. However, if you are a career author looking to create a high-quality print book that meets industry standards, we don't recommend using a conversion service.

With free conversion services, you'll have very little ability to customize the text. If you don't like how a sentence splits across a line or a chapter break, you can't fix it. You're also limited in design elements, like font choices and images, so the books can sometimes look bland. Of course, that's not a problem in e-book formats because the e-reader typically adjusts the format to suit the user's preferences, anyway. However, it can be a bigger problem for print, especially hardback editions, if readers expect a more unique design.

In addition, these services are more likely to result in accidental errors or conversion problems in the text. If you choose this option, make sure you review all your files carefully before you click that publish button. Still, this is a good option for faster production at zero financial cost.

Vellum

If you're willing to spend a little money and plan to publish several books, Vellum is a step up from the free conversion programs. It's a software that will format your book in all formats with more customization and artistic flair, and it doesn't break the bank. At the time of this writing, you'll pay $250 for lifetime access to create unlimited e-books and print books. It's also incredibly easy to use. Megan formatted her most recent release with Vellum in about thirty minutes.

That said, it works best for fiction or narrative nonfiction—anything without charts or graphs or multiple images. For more complicated jobs, your best bet is to hire a professional.

HIRE SOMEONE

The last formatting option is to hire someone to do the work for you, which can cost as little as $15 or more than $1,000. The vast price range will have to do with the experience level of the pro and the complexity of the project.

On the cheaper end, you'll hire someone to use their Vellum software to create your book. This will save you time, and it will also save you money in the short term. If you're a bucket-lister or writing nonfiction, this very well may be the way you want to go. It's cheap and easy, and you'll end up with a good-quality book. You can find these kinds of formatters on Fiverr.com.

However, if you're a career author writing a long series, you may prefer to do it on your own. Not only will you eventually make back the cost of the software in saved fees, you'll also control your files and won't have to pay extra to make changes if you find typos or other errors after publication.

If you're publishing a coffee-table book or limited edition hardcover, or if you have a lot of charts, tables, or specialty formatting issues, spend some extra cash to hire someone skilled in InDesign—a more complex software. These designers will charge anywhere from a few hundred to over a thousand, depending on the complexity of the project.

If you hire someone for a more complicated layout, make sure you have a clear picture of what you want the final product to look like before they start work. This will save money on edits and changes to the final formatting. Late stage changes can quickly add up.

Finding Service Providers

A great way to find service providers is to return to your genre research. Look at books similar to your own. If you like the cover design, or if it seems well edited, consider hiring those providers. Most books, especially those by indie authors, include the editor's and cover designer's information on the copyright page.

If you don't find anyone you like there, don't be afraid to ask around your writing community. If you've done your homework, you should already be building a network of other writers you can reach out to for referrals. Similarly, many online groups will publish a list of recommended service providers including freelance editors, cover designers, formatters, and more.

Conferences are another excellent source for both networking and finding service providers, especially editors. Many of the editors you'll meet at these events take freelance jobs. Then of course, there's the standard Google search. It's harder to know who to trust, but you can often review portfolios and client testimonials online, so it's worth the effort.

Connecting with Service Providers

Once you've found someone you think you'd like to work with, you must contact them. This isn't as common sense as it first seems. Just as there's a protocol for querying an agent, there's a protocol for querying service providers as well.

However, before you contact them, you'll want to read through their references and look through their entire portfolio to make sure their work fits your needs. Editors should have a list of clients they've worked with, along with testimonials. Cover artists should have an online gallery of their designs. Look for freelancers who work in your genre; a cover designer who specializes in thrillers might not be the best choice for nonfiction.

If the service provider doesn't list references online, don't be afraid to ask. Then take the extra step and contact the references to find out whether they enjoyed working with that person or if they had problems. An artist may create beautiful covers but is notoriously late, or doesn't know how to take criticism, or nickels and dimes clients for every change.

When you're ready to make the first contact, it's important to put your best foot forward. Many service providers, especially the good ones, are selective about their projects. But even if they're not picky, it's a good idea to share some basic information about your project to help them assess if the book is a good fit for their style.

Read the submission guidelines on their website if they have them. Follow the instructions to the letter. We cannot state this enough. Some service providers may want an email, others use a submission form. Some may want a specific list of information, others leave it open-ended. Double and triple check before hitting send. They may decline to work with you if you can't follow instructions, or worse, they might not see your query at all.

If the service provider doesn't have submission guidelines, here are some things you may want to include in your email:

- Personal introduction
- The reason you're contacting them
- Who referred you (if a referral)
- What drew your attention to their work
- A brief (couple of sentences) synopsis of your project, including the genre
- For editors: the manuscript length
- Desired project start and end dates

Don't be afraid to ask for more information about their process. You should feel very comfortable before shelling out hundreds or thousands of dollars. Remember, this is a business deal which means you should have a written contract, or at least an email that lays out the terms of your agreement. The contract or written communication should include project start dates, end dates, payment schedules, and cancellation terms. Make sure you're happy with everything before committing.

In addition, before paying a thousand dollars or more for a full edit of your manuscript, it might make sense to request a test edit. Many editors will offer a free sample edit or special pricing to review a small sample of your work—usually the first chapter up to the first fifty pages. The test edit will give you a good idea of the quality of their work and whether you enjoy working with them. If they don't list a sample edit option on their website, ask.

Which leads us to an important warning. As you're researching and finding potential service providers, be careful. Don't be afraid to ask questions and think critically about the services you're hiring. Our good friend and fellow author, Jeffrey J. Michaels, likes to say, "There are more people making money on writers, than writers making money on writing." Unfortunately, we agree.

There are many predatory people hunting for uninformed

writers. There are companies that will offer to publish your book for a mere ten thousand dollars, then do nothing more than give you an inexperienced editor and stock cover design. There are promotion companies that will—for just two hundred dollars—tweet your book five times a day for a week to their hundred thousand followers who may or may not be interested in reading anything, let alone buying your book.

So before you make a deal, consider the quality of your end product and your potential return on investment. How many books do you have to sell just to break even?

GETTING THE MOST FROM YOUR TEAM

The relationship between the independent publisher and their team differs from traditionally published authors' relationships with their teams. You're footing the bill, so you are the client. You're also the boss.

You must be sure you're getting what you need. Politely request changes and edits understanding that often the service provider knows more than you do. He or she can produce a better project if you have an open mind and a hands-off attitude.

When Megan was working with a cover designer on the second book in *The Sanyare Chronicles*, she wasn't thrilled with the model's pose. On the first book's cover there was a sense of action, of movement, but on the new one, it felt static. Megan politely requested a different pose.

The designer responded with a link to the photo series available. It quickly became clear there wasn't a better option. The photographer who had taken the photos had done about a hundred-fifty poses with the chosen model in the outfit they needed. Only about five or six would work. The fact was, the designer had chosen the best pose for the second cover.

Demanding impossible changes will cause subpar results.

Step back and try to be objective. Even if something doesn't match what you have in your head, it might be the best choice. In Megan's case, the designer—who'd created hundreds of covers—knew better than she did what would work for her book. Go figure.

A Note on Speed to Market

If you're an avid follower of other independent writers, you've probably heard stories of authors who write and publish a full-length novel every year, twice a year, every month, even a trilogy in eight weeks.

We're going to let you in on a little secret: most of those authors have been writing and publishing for a long time. Many of them write as their full-time career. Don't compare yourself to them. It might be a goal to strive for, but don't let it push you to produce less than your best work.

From a marketing perspective, the faster you publish, the more money you're going to make. It's true, if only because with each new book, you have a new product for sale. Add on the compounding effect of momentum, and publishing fast can have significant benefits. But if you have a full-time job and family responsibilities, you're probably not going to write that quickly and still produce a quality book.

It's easy to rush the publication process because there's no one to slow you down. But just because you *can,* doesn't mean you *should.* Quality trumps quantity. Reputation matters. If you want to build an audience of raving fans, you have to first focus on the craft. As you get better and publish more, your speed will improve. However, with those first few books in particular, a steady, intentional process can improve the potential of your story and reduce negative feedback.

The unfortunate fact of the matter is that you can't avoid criticism and rejection by avoiding the traditional pitching process; they're part of the writer's experience. In fact, in some ways, indies have it worse. While agents and editors might reject a manuscript, at least those rejections aren't public record. Reviews are. By going through the editorial process and taking your time to get the cover design and formatting right, you'll be minimizing public rejection.

Note, we said minimize, not avoid. Although every writer's journey is unique, we've never met a single one who didn't have a negative review, a nasty critique, or a heartbreaking disappointment. However, if you've done everything possible to ensure your product is professional, it will be easier to deal with criticism when it comes.

PRINT AND DISTRIBUTION OPTIONS

The final step in the publishing process is to upload your book onto an online sales platform. Each distribution option has its own set of quirks and ninja tricks. There are books and courses and instructors who have spent the time to become true experts in each. We'll give you the basics here, starting with the biggest and most well-known of the sales platforms.

Amazon

Kindle Direct Publishing, also known as KDP, is the self-publishing platform for Amazon books. Every independent author will want to sell their books on Amazon. It always makes sense to go directly to them for sales. As an indie, you'll sell most (if not all) of your books on that platform. By uploading directly to Kindle rather than using a service like Smashwords (more on that below) you'll earn the largest royalty possible.

To start, visit KDP.Amazon.com and login with your existing Amazon password, or create a new account. Amazon will walk you through the rest. It's fairly self-explanatory. You'll fill out an online form, upload your cover and interior files, and click submit. It will take a few days, but after Amazon has completed its content review process, you'll have a book available for sale in the Kindle store.

However, there is one more important decision to make before you upload onto the Amazon platform: Do you want to put your book in Kindle Unlimited by checking the box for KDP Select—or not?

Kindle Unlimited is the subscription reading program for the Amazon Kindle. Readers pay a monthly fee for unlimited borrows of books within the program. It's a great deal for the voracious readers who tear through multiple books in a month, or a week, or even a day sometimes.

From the author's side, all you have to do to put your book in Kindle Unlimited is to check the box for KDP Select. The names are a little confusing, but Kindle Unlimited is the reading program, and KDP Select is the author program that feeds into Kindle Unlimited. There are both conditions and benefits to joining KDP Select.

When you sign up for KDP Select, you agree to a minimum ninety-day term of e-book exclusivity in the Amazon store that will auto-renew every ninety days until you uncheck the box. This means you can't sell your e-book anywhere else. Not Apple. Not on your own website. Nowhere else but Amazon until you opt out of the program and finish your latest term. If you break the rules, you could be axed from the Amazon platform entirely.

The benefit, however, is that the Kindle Unlimited pool of readers is massive. Some subscribers will read through an entire series in a day. But if you're not a part of Kindle Unlimited, they probably won't even look at your book. To some extent, the Kindle Unlimited audience is separate from the paid book audience. So if you want to reach those voracious readers—if that's your target market—then you must be in the program.

As the author, you're paid out of a pool of money that is assessed by Amazon each month. Each author receives a share of that pool based on the number of pages read from their books. Therefore, the payout rate changes each month depending on how many total pages were read in Kindle Unlimited that month and how many pages were read from your books.

Besides gaining access to Kindle Unlimited, another benefit to the KDP Select program is the ability to run special pricing promotions on your book that are not available to non-KDP Select authors. This can make it a lot easier to gain visibility and reach readers on the Amazon platform, especially for authors with only a few books available for sale.

The downside to all this is that you're losing all potential sales on other sites. This is especially painful in the international markets like Canada and Europe, where Kobo holds a big market share. In some countries, Kobo's is even larger than Amazon's. Plus, many people fear becoming dependent on one distributor.

If you're just starting out and publishing your very first book, it may be a good idea to join KDP Select. It limits the publishing and sales learning curve to one platform, and when you only have one book available for sale, it's more difficult to promote your books on the non-Amazon sites.

However, once you have three or more books available for sale, especially in a series, you have more marketing options on the non-Amazon platforms and it may be worthwhile to consider taking those books wide, or out of Kindle Unlimited.

We'll talk more about marketing and promotions in future books and courses. For now, it's good to know that these options exist so you can think about what you want for your book. And remember: you're an indie, which means you can always change your mind, pivot, and try something new.

Non-Amazon Platforms

If you decide not to join the KDP Select program, there are several companies to look into for what's commonly known as "wide" distribution.

Aggregators

The easiest way to distribute e-books is through e-book aggregators. The two most common of these are Smashwords and Draft2Digital. You upload your e-book files to one site, and that aggregator distributes it to the sales platforms of your choice, including Amazon, Apple, and Barnes & Noble, amongst many others. They are a great way to reach wider markets, especially internationally. However, they also take a percentage of your royalties on top of whatever the sales platforms take. For example, by publishing directly to Amazon, you would earn 70% of each sale, but Draft2Digital would keep an additional 10%, leaving you with 60% of each sale. For some people, the convenience of having a single place to track and manage e-book sales is worth the reduced royalty rate.

Direct Platforms

Most career independent authors go directly to the major platforms to maximize their earnings. These may include Amazon, Apple, Kobo, and Barnes & Noble. Each of these sites has their own requirements for upload and distribution, but you will always earn more on each sale if you go direct. In addition, you might capitalize on better promotional opportunities.

Print Distribution

If you are interested in publishing your book in paperback, there are two primary options: print on demand or a print run at a printing press.

For most independent authors, print on demand is the preferred method. Paperbacks are typically a tiny percentage of overall indie author sales, and we rarely have the capital necessary to buy hundreds or thousands of books up-front. Then there are the storage problems. Will you have to rent a storage unit? Keep dozens of heavy boxes in your garage? It can be a hassle.

Print on demand companies take care of that problem by only printing the exact number of books you need, when you need them. Plus, they have relationships with most of the major bookstores and online sales platforms, so a customer can order the book online and it will be printed and shipped that same day with no involvement from the author.

The two main print on demand companies are KDP Print, which, as you can probably tell, is an Amazon company and is accessed via the same KDP publishing portal you would use for e-books. And IngramSpark, which is more commonly used by small presses and may have better distribution to non-Amazon bookstores and libraries . . . maybe. Both options are good for what they are and the cost is about the same, so which one you choose may come down to preference.

Calling-card authors may want to look into other printing options. If you plan to sell your books at large events—like speaking engagements, conferences or conventions—or if you plan to give your books away to potential clients, you'll want to get your per unit cost as low as possible. This will increase your profit margins. By ordering in bulk from a printing press— we're talking several hundred or even thousand books—you'll get the best possible pricing. You must do some research to find one that meets your needs, but the effort will be worth it if this is your sales model.

TO RECAP

Complete a **Self-Inventory**. A worksheet has been included in the Pro-Author Packet, which you can download for free by visiting www.AuthorWheel.com/ProAuthor and joining our list.

Editors:

- Developmental editors work on story structure
- Copyeditors work on language and style
- Proofreaders find typos and format errors
- Acquisition editors work for publishing houses

Covers:

- Premade covers are the least expensive
- Custom photo manipulation covers are moderately priced
- Fully illustrated covers are the most expensive

Formatting:

- Do-it-yourself formatting requires tech savvy and patience, but is free
- Free conversion services give you the least flexibility, but they're simple
- Vellum is a formatting software that gives you more flexibility for a one time fee
- Hiring a pro is the easiest, but can ultimately be the most costly

Print and Distribution Options:

Amazon is the biggest platform and you upload your books through their Kindle Direct Publishing website (www.KDP. Amazon.com). From there, you can choose to join KDP Select to have your books included in the Kindle Unlimited reading program. However, if you put your books in KDP Select they can only be sold on Amazon.

If you choose to go "wide" with your books, aggregators can be helpful, however you'll make less money per unit sold than if you go direct to the sales platforms

Print on Demand is the preferred method of print publishing

for most indie authors. The two primary companies used for this are KDP Print and Ingram Spark.

Calling-card writers may want to consider larger print runs from a small printing press.

Chapter Six
Pitching and Selling Your Work

Don't skip this chapter!

Many writers dislike the word marketing. For most, the marketplace is foreign territory. New writers (and some longtime ones) don't know how to prepare for it, nor what to say when they get there. You probably came to writing as a creative endeavor because you wanted to tell stories, not because you wanted to sell them. This may have led you toward traditional publishing under the impression that you won't have to. The truth is, even traditionally published authors need to sell their work, they just have a different first buyer.

In the context of this chapter, the marketplace isn't only Amazon or Barnes and Noble. The marketplace is also the conference where you intend to pitch your work to agents. The marketplace can be an acquisition editor's inbox. So whether you are planning to publish independently or to seek a traditional deal, you're not getting out of this marketing thing.

It doesn't have to be painful, however. Taking your goods to the marketplace can be a fun and creative endeavor—if you're ready. Preparation is the difference between a positive experience and a humiliating one.

But . . . but . . . Winona Writer, your critique partner, had a fabulous manuscript and didn't even get a nibble at your local area conference. And Ira Indie published his fantastic sci-fi novel on Amazon, and the only one who purchased it was his mother.

A polished manuscript is just the baseline. It's what's expected of everyone in the publishing arena. Your job now is to get people past the title page.

This is where presentation comes in. Good presentation includes describing your book in concise, intriguing language and for the indie author, presenting yourself as a professional publisher.

There are many ingredients in the book marketing package, and we're going to go over many of them in this chapter. Let's start with a tiny yet powerful one, the logline.

THE LOGLINE

A logline is a brief, one sentence description of your story. Movie studios use them in their marketing materials, businesses call them 'elevator pitches.' Loglines are essential for catching an agent's, editor's, or reader's attention. Think of them as the bait on your query fishing pole.

Going through the process of writing a logline also helps you understand the core element of your book so you can write or talk about it intelligently. Unfortunately, although they are so much shorter than your manuscript, many writers feel they're harder to write. Let's try to simplify the process. Start by asking yourself these questions.

- Who is my story about?
- What does he/she want that he/she doesn't have?
- What's stopping him/her from getting it?
- Where does the story take place?

The first question is typically the easiest. For nonfiction

authors, particularly self-help authors, this may be the reader, or in the case of a memoir, it would you. For fiction authors, it is your main character. Not the character's name, but their occupation, situation, etc. We want the reason you chose this protagonist. Highlight a piece of their personality, and what makes them unique from other protagonists in your genre.

As an example, we're going to walk through the creation of Greta's logline for her first book, *A Margin of Lust*. She received a contract from a Twitter pitch event with the final product.

Her story is about an ambitious real estate agent.

The next two questions work together. If your character or reader doesn't want something they can't seem to get, you don't have conflict. If you don't have conflict, you don't have a story or a nonfiction book. It's back to the drawing board.

In *A Margin of Lust*, Greta's character wants to sell the beach front property she just listed. She wants prestige and success. But every time she puts the place on the market, something goes horribly wrong.

Question four is optional. You only need to mention the setting if it applies to the story or to the theme. Greta mentions the town her book takes place in, or Southern California, because she advertises her series as:

Ordinary women. Unexpected evil. A taut psychological suspense series that exposes the dark side of sunny Southern California.

Southern California is a main character in her stories.

For nonfiction, you want to express the reader's problem. For example, if you're writing a book about how to organize your kitchen, you'll want to highlight the specific issues your target reader is dealing with. Are they tired of searching for cooking tools? Do they want efficiency, but can't seem to achieve it? In this case, you only have to mention the place as it relates to the book. Is it about apartment kitchens, small kitchens, upscale kitchens, industrial kitchens, or all of the above?

Back to the *Margin of Lust* logline, the answer to the last question is Laguna Beach. So putting the above together we get:

A real estate agent's new oceanfront Laguna Beach listing is perfect, except for what's hidden in the basement and the body in the upstairs bedroom.

This logline earned Greta five requests for queries, which turned into two requests for full manuscripts, which turned into a contract for the first two books in the series and first right of refusal on the other five.

You can see that sometimes what the protagonist wants is implied, not direct, but you, the author, need to know what that is. The real estate agent wants to sell the house, obviously. That's why the listing is perfect. Why can't she? Because there's some crazy stuff happening in that house.

Some Famous Examples

A police chief with a phobia for open water battles a gigantic shark with an appetite for swimmers and boat captains, in spite of a greedy town council who demands that the beach stay open.[2]

This is, of course, *Jaws*. In this example, we learn a bit more about the police chief—the main character—he has an open water phobia. Why is this important? Well, next we learn what he wants. He wants to stop a gigantic shark from eating people. The phobia is one thing that will hinder his goal. It adds tension to an already tense situation. That the greedy town council demands the beach stay open adds even more conflict.

And another:

An orphaned boy enrolls in a school of wizardry, where he learns the truth about himself, his family, and the terrible evil that haunts the magical world.[3]

In this example from *Harry Potter and the Sorcerer's Stone*, we learn that Harry is an orphan. This is important because it implies that he wants connection, a family, parents, security, all the things children want but orphans don't have. Instead of finding a happy new family, he finds the secret behind his past and a terrible evil. It sets us up for both this story and the books that are to come. We know, even if we'd never heard of Harry Potter, that he'll be the one to save the world.

One more:

This book will teach you the secrets that could bring you a fortune.

This line is in the description of Napoleon Hill's *Think and Grow Rich* on Amazon's website. It's a pretty powerful promise, and it certainly helped to make him rich. The reader's problem is implied again—he or she isn't rich, but they want to be.

Now that you've seen some examples, use the answers to the questions you wrote and try writing your own logline. You can use a format like this to get started:

A (career and/or something else interesting about your protagonist/reader) from (where the story takes place if pertinent) wants (what they want) but (what's stopping them from getting it.)

Play with this sentence, reorganize it, swap the pieces around until you have four or five possibilities. Now share those with other writers or, even better, in a Twitter Pitch event. (We discussed Twitter Pitches in Chapter Four.)

The wonderful thing about the Twitter Pitch process, whether or not it gets you a publishing deal, is it forces you to distill your story into about 140 characters. Then you see which of those distillations gets attention, if any. If one gets more likes than the rest, or any likes, you're on the right track.

If there are no Twitter Pitches on the horizon and you want feedback on your logline, writers' Facebook groups are great places to post your options.

BOOK DESCRIPTION BASICS

You only have seconds to grab people's attention. It's a simple fact. Once you've gotten them to stop and talk or to click on your cover or open your email, it's imperative to pique their interest. To do that, you need a solid book description.

Book descriptions are what you find on the back cover of a novel, or on the online seller's page next to your front cover. However, even if you're planning to pitch your work to publishers, writing a blurb is an excellent exercise. The better you are at synthesizing your book into talking points, the better you'll be at presenting it to agents and future readers.

There are some universally accepted components to a book description, although there are different "formulas" out there to choose from. There are also differences between writing a book blurb for sales purposes and writing a synopsis for an agent.

Let's start with the ingredients of a book blurb.

- A tagline
- An introduction of the character and/or current state of affairs
- The presentation of the conflict and the stakes (fiction and memoir) or the problems that will be solved (nonfiction, self-help)
- An appeal to genre tropes (optional)
- A call to action (optional)

The tagline is much like the logline, but less explanatory and more emotionally driven. A tagline should be short and concise and use powerful words. It needs to convey the emotion or theme of the story and represent at least one of the main genre tropes readers are looking for. It can be a sentence fragment, single words, or trail off in an ellipsis, but the important thing is it should make the reader want to find out more.

You've already distilled your story down into a single logline, so it's easiest to start from there. Let's look at Greta's logline as the example again:

A real estate agent's new oceanfront Laguna Beach listing is perfect, except for what's hidden in the basement and the body in the upstairs bedroom.

What emotion are we trying to portray? What keywords can we use to describe that emotion as concisely as possible?

A Margin of Lust is a psychological thriller with a dead body in a house for sale. Fear and mystery are the two primary drivers of the story. Remember, for the tagline, we don't need to mention the character or the plot. We're focused on the emotion and the theme of the story. So Greta's tagline became:

Sometimes it's best to leave a door closed.

In that single sentence, we know that a house or a room is critical to the setting. We know that something scary and intriguing is behind that door, and it makes us want to find out what it is, even if we're afraid to turn that knob (or that page.)

In Megan's epic fantasy, *Forged in Shadow*, her theme was that of the average person rising to the occasion to become a hero. She wanted to emphasize that heroes are not born to greatness; they choose it. Her tagline is:

In the chaos of war, not all heroes shine. Some must rise from shadows to claim the light.

For a short story she wrote for an anthology, she chose a tagline that seemed contradictory, but intriguing:

Protector, Champion . . . Oathbreaker

Like the logline, you'll probably have to go through many iterations of your tagline to find the one that fits. Be patient and ask for others' opinions once you have a few for them to compare. You can use Twitter pitch events to test these as well.

After you've grabbed the reader's attention with your tagline, you need to make them care. Fiction and nonfiction writers will approach this differently.

Fiction authors often want to spell out the plot of their book in the blurb but, believe it or not, this isn't the place for it. For one thing, it would be a spoiler. For another, fiction is about living in someone else's shoes for a while. It's an escape into another reality. The reader doesn't so much care about what's going to happen; they want to relate to the character and enter their world. For that reason, your description should begin by introducing your character and the current state of affairs as the book opens.

Once you've established your character, you want to highlight the emotional drivers and primary conflict of the story. What's the problem that the protagonist must overcome? What changes are they going to have to make? What are the stakes if they don't solve that problem?

These are all good questions for the nonfiction author to ponder as well, but in nonfiction the reader is the protagonist. Tell them what they'll learn if they read the book. How will it change their life? Apply the WIIFM principle for the reader: *What's in it for me?*

You might write a synopsis of chapter topics, or a success story from someone who applied your wisdom, or how you learned what you wrote about and how it impacted your life.

The body of the description is typically no more than two or three paragraphs, but nonfiction writers might also include bulleted lists as appropriate. No matter what you're writing, make sure you go back again to your market research to see what styles of descriptions are working for the bestsellers in your genre.

Before we move on, let's take a moment to discuss fiction novels that include more than one protagonist. No matter how many point of view characters you have, your book description should focus on only two major characters, and each should have their own separate paragraph.

The first paragraph should be about the primary character who carries the story. The second paragraph could be the love interest or another character who is integral to the plot, but still secondary to the primary character. If you include any more than that—even if they're important to the plot—you'll overwhelm your reader and probably lose the sale.

Finally, you might appeal to your genre's tropes. If you're wondering what the heck we are talking about, we can guarantee you've seen this done. This is the sentence or two toward the bottom of the book description that either compares the book to other authors' books or uses action words to identify the subgenre to readers. For example:

If you love action-packed stories filled with myth, magic, and mayhem, you'll love this fantasy adventure by Megan Haskell.

Action-packed, myth, magic, and mayhem are all words associated with fantasy adventure. It's what readers of the genre want.

If you enjoyed The Girl Before *by JP Delaney and* Behind Closed Doors *by BA Paris, you'll be taken captive by this twisty, psychological suspense story by Greta Boris.*

These are popular books in the same vein as *A Margin of Lust* by Greta. It's a way of letting readers know about the world they'll be entering. Add in the "taken captive" and "twisty" and you know you're in for an exciting story.

You could also compare a nonfiction book to other nonfiction books that cover the same type of material, as long as you're not competing with them for sales. Keep in mind, this part of the description is optional. Some authors hate using it, but others swear it helps make the sale.

Finally, another optional but possibly useful element of a book description—at least on Amazon sales pages—is the final call to action. This is the last line of your description, and it essentially asks the reader to buy the book. It doesn't have to be quite so blunt, but something like:

- *Enter the world of [fill in the blank] today!*
- *Start your journey . . .*
- *Be swept away . . .*

- *Or for nonfiction: Don't wait, solve your problem now!*

Spend some time reading the descriptions of the bestsellers in your genre. Think about how they're similar, and what they do differently. What grabs your attention? Then write at least three to five versions of your own and ask for feedback from other authors and readers of your genre before making any final decisions.

Writing a solid book description can be time-consuming and difficult. Like everything else, it's an art unto itself. But the reward is well worth the effort.

THE FORMAL BOOK SYNOPSIS

The dreaded synopsis, unlike a book blurb, actually does talk about the plot of your story, but most authors still hate writing them. Hopefully, we can break it down into manageable steps to make it a little less painful.

A synopsis is a required element of the query letter, but even if you're planning to independently publish, this is a good writing exercise. It helps you clarify the major plot points of your story. In fact, some people write them before they write their book to keep themselves on track while drafting, sort of like an outline. Others—more often 'pantsers' or 'discovery writers'—will write them after the fact to help guide their revision efforts.

Synopses come in three standard lengths. When you're getting ready to pitch agents and editors, you should probably have all three prepared. However, each length can build upon the others.

The shortest synopsis is two to three paragraphs. This is the one you'll include in your actual query letter. It is very similar to a back cover book description, but there are a few key differences.

First, you will include more plot in the synopsis, though it's still not a complete plot outline. Instead, focus on what makes your story different. Give us the where and how and who, not so much the what.

For example: A dying man makes a deal with the devil. This is a familiar trope. From *Faust* to *The Devil and Daniel Webster* to Kingsolver's *Poisonwood Bible*, more writers than we can list have tackled it.

But what if we say: A dying man learns to cook meth to provide for his family after he's gone and ends up in a relationship with a drug lord he can't escape from.

This is *Breaking Bad*, of course. You can see that the basic plot isn't anything new. What is new is where and how and who must deal with this age-old dilemma.

You'll also want to give the reader a peek into your characters' personalities. What are the key traits that set them apart from other people? What's their problem? Talk a bit about the world they're living in, and how they resolve their dilemma. If you have dueling protagonists, you'll need to mention both.

Here's an example of a short synopsis for a Women's Fiction novel with two protagonists Greta co-authored with another writer.

Candace St. John, a stay-at-home-mom, like Mary Poppins, is practically perfect in every way. Okay, she's a bit controlling, but when no one else knows how to get things done, what's she supposed to do? Mara Lewis, manager of the local garden center, is too busy to stick her shovel into other people's dirt, and she'd rather they stay out of hers.

When a threatening photo of Candace's son and a new girl in town shows up on Candace's windshield, her carefully constructed life begins to crack. When that same girl, an employee at the nursery, tells Mara she might be pregnant, a fissure opens in the wall surrounding Mara's heart.

The child could be Candace's grandchild. It could be the answer to Mara's prayers. It can't be both. The two women, despite their mutual dislike, delve into secrets and lies to uncover an enemy that could destroy both their families. When the threats mount, their fragile friendship provides the answers.

In this example we know right away who these women are, and the implied conflict between them. But these diametrically opposed personalities are going to have to join forces to face an enemy and solve the mystery behind the photo. In three paragraphs, we've described our characters, their present situation, future conflict, personal stakes, and potential conclusion.

The tone of the synopsis should reflect the tone of the book, but not be written in the exact voice of the characters. For example, in this synopsis there is subtle humor, Candace is controlling, but what can she do when she's the only one who knows how to get anything done? And there's a gardening pun in Mara's description. The reader can also tell this is a heartwarming story thanks to references to things like walls around hearts and answers to prayers. Words like enemy, destroy, secrets, lies, and threats give a sense of the danger the characters will face.

One final note: the synopsis should be written in the present tense, even if the book is written in past tense. For that matter, most back-cover book descriptions are also written in the present tense. It gives immediacy to the blurb and will be expected by agents and acquisitions editors.

After you've written the short synopsis, it's time to move onto the one-page synopsis. In this version, you give the reader more plot. It's less of a teaser and more of a road map through the book. You'll need to describe each point of basic story structure.

- The opening hook – the protagonists state at the beginning of the story
- The conflict – what they want that's being withheld from them

- Their cross over threshold – the point at which they decide to go after what they want
- Try/fail cycles (or try/succeed) – what happens when they do
- The mirror moment – their ah-ha moment when they realize they've been looking at things all wrong
- The grand battle – where they confront the antagonist, the point where all is lost or won
- The denouement – the story resolution

Start by writing two or three sentences for each of the above pieces of your story's structure. Here are a couple of examples from Greta's novella *Mortuary School.*

Opening hook: Imogene Lynch, a twenty-something rockabilly hair stylist has decided on an unusual career change because of a gift (some say curse) she's recently discovered. When she touches the hair of the deceased, she's barraged by the last emotions that person experienced. Imogene enrolls in the Cavendish School of Mortuary Science with the goal of becoming just an ordinary mortician.

The conflict: She doesn't understand, nor does she embrace her hair-sensitivity. On her first day of class, two corpses are discovered in a casket that should only contain one. Imogene is shoved forward and inadvertently touches the hair of one of the dead bodies. She's rocked by emotions.

And so on. You'll find this helps you to highlight the important plot points, so you don't get lost in the weeds.

The tone of the longer form synopsis is less important than the clarity. If you can throw in a bit of clever phrasing, that's fine, but don't focus on it. Like the short synopsis, it should be written in present tense.

When you're done with your outline, either edit or expand it depending on what you need. If you're asked for a one-page synopsis, you might need to combine a couple of the above major plot points. When writing a three-page synopsis, you may need to give more detail.

Another thing writers worry about is giving away the ending. Don't. Agents and editors don't want to be surprised. They're not concerned about spoilers. They want to see that your story has a clearly thought-out plot with a satisfying and logical conclusion before they spend the time reading the manuscript.

When you're done, it's always a good plan to have someone else read your synopsis to see if it makes sense to them. If not, you might need to do some adjusting.

ISBNS, KEYWORDS, AND PRICING

This section is a bit of a mish-mash of concepts that indie authors will need to consider before publishing their first book, but we believe even traditionally published authors should understand the ins and outs of actually putting your book for sale on an online platform. Having a better understanding of the market and the sales process will show that you're taking your writing career seriously and are considering the best ways to reach your audience.

That said, all three of these topics have entire books written about them. It's out of the scope of this book to go into that much detail. Our intention is to get you started with the basics. You can figure out the details and play with your strategies later.

First, the ISBN. What is it?

The ISBN is the number, like a UPC code, that identifies your book. It is used across all platforms and allows bookstores and libraries to find, sell, and track data about your specific book, including the title, author, publisher, and sales details.

Some e-book aggregators, like Kindle Publishing, Smashwords, and Draft2Digital, will give you a free ISBN when you publish with their service. This is a great option for bucket-listers or dabblers who aren't planning to publish more than one book. If you choose this option, Kindle, Smashwords or Draft2Digital will be the "publisher of record," which means their name will appear on the publisher line of the online retailers. (If you need a refresher on the different sales platforms, go back to Chapter Five.)

Some authors feel that having a generic publisher of record looks unprofessional. Instead, they suggest you create your own publishing company, buy ISBNs, and list that company name as the publisher. If you choose this route, you can buy ISBNs from Bowker (www.myidentifiers.com).

However, ISBNs aren't cheap unless you buy them in bulk. At the time of this writing, one ISBN costs $125, ten cost $295, and 100 cost $575. And you'll need a different ISBN for each format of your book: e-book, paperback, hardback, audio . . . each one needs its own tracking number, so it quickly adds up. For example, if you're writing a five book series and planning to release both e-book and paperback, you'll need ten ISBNs before publication.

If you're an entrepreneur, calling-card writer, or an artist with plans of making a career writing, consider this option. It can provide more legitimacy to your work, help identify you as a serious author-publisher, and ensure that your book sales are appropriately tracked.

Plus, once you've used an ISBN for a book, you cannot reuse it, nor can you change it. If you decide you don't want to use the Smashwords ISBN any longer, you'll have to unpublish the book and release it as a new title—even if everything else stays the same.

No matter what you choose to do, an ISBN will be required for publication, so have the decision made and the number ready to go (if you're going to buy your own).

Keywords

Keywords are words or phrases that readers use to search for books and online retailers use to identify their subject matter. When you upload your book to Amazon or another retailer, you'll be asked to provide between five and ten words or phrases describing your book.

There are a few things to keep in mind as you choose your keywords. First, you can use more than a single word per entry. In fact, some authors follow a strategy called "keyword stuffing" where they try to put as many relevant words into each keyword entry box as possible. Others prefer to think of specific terms or phrases that their target readers will type into the search box.

You'll also want to avoid repeating yourself. You don't want to include the same term multiple times in different boxes. Try to be creative and think of alternate ways of saying the same thing. For example; female protagonist, strong heroine, or woman warrior.

For the same reason, you'll want to avoid using primary genre categories as a single word keyword, like "Thriller" or "Fantasy." You'll select these separately during the upload process and they'll carry over into search terms as well. Instead, try to be as specific as possible and think about what your target audience is looking for.

For example, some of Megan's keyword phrases for *The Sanyare Chronicles* include "kick-ass heroine", "elves fae and mythological creatures," and "action adventure fantasy with a female lead."

There are a few services that can help identify good keywords, but when you're first launching your book we suggest you just spend an hour or so brainstorming as many keywords and keyword phrases as you can think of. After you've gotten your first book out there, you can always do more research and adjust (or optimize) your terms to increase your visibility or trigger the sales algorithms.

Pricing

Last, but not least, as an indie, you have to decide how much you want to charge for your book. There are several pricing strategies to consider.

We'll start with e-books. To get the best royalty rate on Amazon Kindle books (70%) you must price your book between $2.99 and $9.99. Anything lower or higher than that, and you'll only earn 35%. You also can't make your book free on Amazon in the beginning. The lowest price you can set by yourself is 99¢.

However, there are two ways you can make your book free on Amazon (and there are several reasons you might do this):

If you choose to join KDP Select, you can opt to run up to seven days free promotion during each ninety day term. This is great for a short-term promotion to boost visibility or generate sales through a series.

You can offer your book for free on another platform and have Amazon match the price.

Most indie authors price their e-books significantly lower than their traditional counterparts. This is because they don't have the overhead of the publishing houses, and since the author is earning most of the retail price, they can afford it. In fact, it's a strategic advantage for indies. Most indies sell their full-priced e-books between $2.99 and $5.99 and more often on the lower side. However, note that if you price your book differently on other sites, Amazon will almost always match the price and you'll get the associated royalty.

If you're planning on publishing a longer series, you might also consider dropping your first book to 99¢ despite the lower royalty rate to encourage readers who've never heard of you to give your book a try. If they like it, you'll make more money on the full-priced books later in the series. Some authors will even give away their first book to draw readers into the series, pricing the rest between $2.99 and $4.99.

Ultimately, your pricing strategy is up to you. Lower prices may generate more unit sales volume, high prices get you more income per book. If you only have one book out, your strategy will be different than if you have a ten book series. Whatever you decide, just remember that you're an indie . . . you can always change your mind!

Print pricing, however, requires a different mindset. Unfortunately, indies in this case do not have a competitive advantage unless they invest in a small print run. The per unit cost of a print-on-demand book is significantly higher than the per unit cost of a print run of several thousand books.

The good news is, there aren't the same royalty price restrictions or guidelines for print as there are for digital books.

When pricing print books, first figure out how much you'd like to earn per book sold. Megan usually tries to give herself a $3 margin. This allows for a little room for sales discounts while still giving her a profit on each book sold.

When you fill out the pricing information on the print-on-demand platform, they will give you the minimum price to break even. They base this price on your production costs (e.g. page count, paper type, cover type, etc.) and the retailers' take. Use that number and add the amount you'd like to make per book to arrive at your sales price.

The sales price isn't the same as your per unit wholesale cost. If you order copies of your own book, you won't pay the retailer's cut. For example, Megan can purchase author copies of *Forged in Shadow* for $6.53 but the minimum price she can sell the book for to break even is $13.33. Since she wants to earn about a $3 margin per sale, she rounds up to the nearest 99¢ and sells the paperback for $16.99. This also allows her to give in-person discounts at events where she sells directly to readers.

Author copy – $6.53

Break-even bookstore price – $13.33

Retail price – $16.99

Price can be a fun element to play with over time. Try one thing for a month or two, and if it's not working, try something else.

TO RECAP

A **logline** is a brief, one sentence description of your story.

Book Descriptions, or blurbs, include:

- A tagline (similar to a logline, but more emotive & less descriptive)
- An introduction of the character and/or current state of affairs
- The presentation of the conflict and the stakes (fiction and memoir) or the problems that will be solved (nonfiction, self-help)
- An appeal to genre tropes (optional)
- A call to action (optional)

Synopses come in three standard lengths: two to three paragraphs, one page and three pages.

An **ISBN** is a number, like a UPC code, that identifies your book. Many e-book distributors will give them to you for free, but you can also buy them for all formats on Bowker at www.myidentifiers.com.

Keywords are words or phrases that readers use to search for books and online retailers use to identify their subject matter.

Pricing e-books requires a different strategy than print books. Most indie authors price their e-books between $2.99 and $5.99. Paperback pricing will depend on the cost to print the book.

Chapter Seven
Managing Your Author Business

One thing we have seen over the years is talented writers who never publish and not-so-talented writers who do. What's the difference? Generally, it's the difference between dreamers and doers. If you've gotten this far in the book, congratulations. We bet you're a doer or on your way to becoming one. If you don't feel you're there yet, we'll help you set SMART goals, create your own deadlines to keep yourself accountable, and get on the path to *your* vision of success.

SET SMART GOALS FOR PUBLISHING

There's a statement that's touted in life coach and business guru circles: if you can imagine yourself doing something, you can achieve it. Is it true?

Scientists from the Cleveland Clinic Foundation in Ohio conducted an interesting experiment.[4] They divided the study into three groups, one did nothing, one visualized pinky exercises, and the third performed physical pinky exercises. Unsurprisingly, the group that performed physical exercises saw a 53 percent increase in strength.

What was a shocker, though, was the group who visualized the exercises saw a 35 percent increase in strength without ever moving a muscle. Before you close the computer, put your feet up and daydream your way through an exercise routine, let's think this through. Why does this work?

Vivid mental images fire neurons in the brain. Those signals travel down the spinal column and enervate the muscles, just like actual experiences do. In fact, many scientists believe your brain can't tell the difference between the two.

Athletes and coaches have used this technique for decades to improve performance. "Visualize the win" is not an uncommon phrase to hear on the court or field. Similarly, psychologists and life coaches often recommend visualizations to help their clients improve their outcomes. Mantras and self-talk are just visualizations with another name.

So why has visualization gotten such bad press recently?

Another study done in New York University's Motivation Lab found daydreams decreased motivation.[5] The people who indulged in fantasies about the cute guy asking them out, or a test paper with a big "A" at the top, were less likely to achieve their dreams. It seems Grandma was correct when she said, "Wish in one hand, spit in the other, and see which gets full first."

Why does visualization work for athletes and not for NYU's student body?

To quote another wise dearly departed, Aristotle, "First, have a definite, clear, practical ideal; a goal, an objective. Second, have the necessary means to achieve your ends: wisdom, money, materials, and methods. Third, adjust all your means to that end."

Too often when writers dream of publishing, that's all they do—dream. They either don't set goals, or their goals are, forgive us, kind of dumb. They don't do the hard work of analyzing the process and creating a realistic, attainable action plan. They either don't have a "clear, practical ideal" or they haven't "adjusted all their means to that end."

Visualization isn't a magic formula, as some would have you believe. It's one ingredient, one tool, to help you achieve your goals. When it comes to creativity and accomplishment, we're often our own worst enemy. What is writer's block if it isn't fear of failure? Why can we find the time to check Facebook forty-five times a day but have no time to finish our query letter? Why does one bad review wipe out the impact of ten positive ones?

We believe premeditated, structured visualization turns your subconscious from enemy to ally. It triggers your brain to work toward a goal. Stephen King calls his muse, "the boys in the basement." It's an apt analogy. Imagine you have a gang sitting at their typewriters chomping cigars, ready to tap out your dictation. What's the story you're telling them to write?

To make it work for you, however, you first must set the goal you want to achieve. Businesses without business plans fail. You may not want to hear it, but these days successful authors embrace the entrepreneurial aspect of their career. Don't think because your goal is to find an agent, you are exempt. You'll be more likely to find and keep an agent if you have this mindset. Whatever path to publication you've chosen to follow, you need SMART goals to keep you on track.

SETTING SMART GOALS

You've probably seen this acronym before, but the best goals are SMART goals:

Specific • Measurable • Attainable • Realistic • Time-bound

This system can apply to any set of goals for any dream you have in your life, but for our purposes we will of course be focusing on your dream of publishing. By walking through this process, you will develop Aristotle's "definite, clear, practical ideal" and ensure that you have the "wisdom, money, materials, and methods" necessary to achieve that ideal.

Let's start from the beginning, with the "S" in SMART. Unless your goals are specific, how can you plan appropriately? How do you know when you've accomplished what you need to accomplish? Hopefully, this will be a simple question for you to answer after working through the first six chapters of this book, but write it down anyway. Written goals are twice as likely to be achieved than unwritten goals according to a study by psychology professor Dr. Gail Matthews.[6]

Examples of Specific Publishing Goals

- I want to publish my own books and become a career indie author.
- I want to find a boutique publisher to publish my finished novel.
- I want to sign with a literary agent and publish my book with a major publisher.

Now that you've written a specific goal, let's make sure it's measurable. Measurable goals have distinct parameters. For instance, in the world of fitness your specific goal might be to run a race. To make that goal measurable, you'd say, I want to run a 5K. Now you know how to train.

Examples of Specific and Measurable Publishing Goals

- I want to independently publish my first book with professional editing and cover design, in both digital and print on demand.
- I want to find a boutique publisher who will create digital versions of my book and will also do print runs and sell my books to bookstores.
- I want to sign with a literary agent who has an excellent

track record selling stories in the genre I write to reputable publishing houses.

When it comes to the "A" in SMART, attainable, people sometimes falter. Writers fear making publishing goals because they feel they have so little control over the process. This is especially true for those seeking outside representation. We get it. There is another person, or people, involved in the process. Finding an agent or a publisher or the perfect independent editor is kind of like finding a spouse. There is uncertainty. But one thing *is* certain, you'll never find what you're looking for if you don't start taking steps in that direction.

If your goal was to run a marathon, for example, and the farthest you'd ever run was a mile, twenty-six miles would feel pretty unattainable. In fact, it *would be* unattainable without training. You would have to break the distance down into small, incremental steps that build on each other. On week one, you push your mile to two. The next week, your goal would be three miles. And so on. Then by the time the race came around, you'd be ready.

By breaking your publishing goal into smaller attainable tasks and conquering each of them one at a time, you'll decrease the feeling of being overwhelmed that often hinders progress. Plus, each minor success will increase your motivation and help you reach the goal.

We suggest you create some steps toward your goal that you do have control over. Think of them as training for the final event—publishing.

Examples of Specific, Measurable, Attainable Publishing Goals

- I'm going to purchase and start learning to use one software program to help me publish my own book.
- I'm going to find and pitch twenty boutique publishers who accept unsolicited manuscripts.

- I am going to find and pitch twenty literary agents who have an excellent track record selling books to major publishers in my genre.

The next two steps of your SMART goal, realistic and time-bound, work together and can be the most uncomfortable to challenge. You must first ask yourself: are you ready to be published? How do you know? Has someone besides your mother read your work and critiqued it? If you've started pitching, have you only received form letters as rejections? How much time can you dedicate to the writing and publishing process?

If you haven't yet assessed the quality of your work—sent it out to beta readers or critique partners and received positive feedback—it might not be realistic to set a goal to publish your book within three months. The critique and editing work must come first.

If your manuscript is polished and ready to go, but you're planning to pursue the agented-traditional path, it's probably not realistic to set a goal to see the book in print within six months when you don't have a publisher yet.

Similarly, if you work full time and have a house full of kids you're shuffling from school to soccer to ballet, recognize there's only so much of you to go around. Writing and publishing takes time no matter which path you pursue. What realistically fits into your schedule?

Writing a novel alone is time consuming. Now add to that working on your craft, researching vendors and publishers, creating a query letter, auditioning editors, starting a website, taking part in social media, and . . . you get the picture.

Realistic goals are going to look different for everyone. You may need to focus on craft for a while, find objective critique partners, and take some writing courses before you're ready to pitch or publish. If your work is ready, but you've never written a query letter or hired a cover designer, you may need to set small realistic goals and complete those tasks before you tackle the next steps.

We've also seen that if we don't set deadlines for our goals, they never happen. Goals are simply dreams with a deadline. And in order to set deadlines without sabotaging ourselves, we must take the entirety of our life into consideration.

Ask yourself: What are you willing to give up? How much time can you dedicate to this process? Where can you find that time? Go back through all the sections of SMART and rewrite your goal with a realistic timeline in mind.

Don't be afraid to reevaluate your goals. The reason New Year's resolutions routinely fail is because they're set once and given little thought. When it becomes obvious they won't happen, people feel like failures and give up. The problem isn't the person, it's the goal. Unrealistic expectations are just that, unrealistic.

Once you have a revised realistic goal in mind, it's time to make it real. Write it down and post it somewhere prominent in your house or at your desk. Then announce it to someone. Share your goals with supportive family and friends, with your writing group, or in your online community.

Why? Because it will help you stay accountable to your dream.

In the next section, we'll show you how to write mini-goals and schedule them on your calendar. Before we do that, however, we have a challenge for you:

Write a brief scene in first person featuring yourself as the main character. Imagine yourself achieving your SMART goal. Where are you? What are you wearing? What do you see, smell, feel, hear? Use your senses.

When you're done, keep this handy and visit it regularly. Read it out loud. This is the visualization we discussed earlier. Its job is to help you achieve those SMART goals.

REVISE YOUR CALENDAR

You've probably figured out by now that setting a goal is not the end of the road. It's only the beginning. The next step is to break the goal into manageable steps and put those steps on the calendar.

We believe the best way to do that is to start with the end: the final deadline. For writers pursuing independent publication, this would be the day of your book launch. For those who choose the traditional publication path, it's the day you want to have your manuscript finished or start sending out query letters. It could also be the deadline for an advanced submission critique at a writers' conference, or the day you have to send your manuscript to a developmental editor.

While you're still writing the first draft, you can keep things a little vague. Something like, "I want to send my first query letter in June" or "I want to publish my book in June." That works . . . until it doesn't. As soon as you hire professionals to work on your project, or register for a conference, you must be more specific. There are two fundamental questions to consider when filling out your calendar:

- How much time will each task require?
- Are there dependencies to the order in which they operate?

For example, there is an order of operations that must occur in the editing process. You must finish your first draft before you send it to beta readers. You must also give beta readers enough time to read and critique your work, typically two to four weeks. Then you must incorporate their suggestions and feedback before you send the manuscript to your editor. The editor will probably take two to four weeks to edit your manuscript, and you can't publish or pitch the book until you've incorporated her suggestions and changes. Each task requires the prior one to be completed before the next can be tackled.

However, there are also tasks that aren't dependent on others' work, like the cover design. If you're an independent author who needs to hire a cover designer, you can do that at any time. In fact, some authors will commission covers before they even write the book. The only dependency is that the cover must be finalized before you submit your files for publication.

For writers pursuing traditional publication, you might write your query while your manuscript is being edited. But you can't send those query letters until the manuscript is complete and as polished as you can make it.

Here are few tasks to consider, grouped by publication path:

Traditional Publishing

- Manuscript preparation
- Beta reader critiques
- Read and review programs
- Professional editing
- Writing the book synopsis
- Conferences
- Query letters

Independent Publishing

- Professional editing
- Cover design
- Formatting
- Writing descriptions
- Filing the copyright
- Scheduling promotions
- Creating teasers and other promotional imagery
- Uploading to distributors: Amazon, KDP, Smashwords, etc.

Obviously, these aren't exhaustive lists. But hopefully it has you thinking about the tasks you need to accomplish to reach your goals.

Once you have a list of tasks, you must figure out approximately how long they'll take, and their order of operation. Then it's time to put them on the calendar.

Let's walk through that process together, using the independent publishing model with a target launch date of June 30 as our example.

Keep in mind, the *process* for creating a timeline is the same for traditional publishing, only the tasks are different. For example, traditionally published authors won't have control over the launch date or have to format their own books. But they will have deadlines for edits and other tasks they can plot on a calendar.

First, write your launch date on your calendar big and bold. Make it red, or circle it, or put a sticker next to it. Your launch date should be prominent, so you never forget what you're working toward.

Next, consider what you need to do immediately prior to your launch date. You'll probably want your book to publish with some positive reviews so potential readers will know it's good. To do that, you'll want to send out advanced reader copies, otherwise known as ARCs, to readers and reviewers in your target audience. These people write reviews for a free copy of the book. They will need enough time to read and prepare a review for the launch day. Let's give them one month. Put May 31st on your calendar as the date to send out the ARCs.

However, in order to send the manuscript to your ARC readers, it must be ready the day before you send it, May 30th. If your formatter requires a week to complete your book, that means you have to have the final copyedited manuscript ready for her by May 23rd.

Prior to that, we need to incorporate the copyeditor's comments. This can take up to a week (maybe more), so the editor must return the book to you by May 16th at the latest.

If the copyeditor needs a month for her work, she'll want to start on April 16th.

Meanwhile, you can work on your book description and cover design. Consider giving yourself deadlines for those things. Your cover designer could start work on April 1, for example. These deadlines might be more flexible than the others, but it's still important to write them down and keep track of them.

The above would look like this:

> April 1 – Book to cover designer
> April 16 – Book to editor
> May 16 – Book back from editor
> May 23 – Manuscript ready for formatter
> May 30 – Book back from formatter
> May 31 – Send ARCs
> **JUNE 30 – Launch!!**

Work on your calendar like this until you have everything plotted out. You might find you need to adjust things as you go, so we recommend using a pencil. Except for the launch date, of course, which should be big and bright and bold and final.

The above is not a comprehensive project plan. Each book launch or major deadline will have unique elements. It is only an example of plotting larger, macro goals by breaking them into micro goals.

The traditional process is the same. Start with the day you want to send out your first query and work backward from there. While the developmental editor has your story, you can write your template query, or assemble a list of agents and small presses you hope to attract.

After you've built out your schedule, don't ignore it. Check the calendar regularly. Review both the day and the month so nothing creeps up on you. Revise the schedule as needed. Add new deadlines and milestones when appropriate. Be flexible, but don't give yourself excuses for not getting your work done.

BUDGET

Regardless of whether you're an independent author-entrepreneur or working with a traditional publisher, you're going to have to consider costs. Yes, the indie method is far more expensive, but even traditional authors have expenses.

Many creatives have a fear of numbers or dislike math, like Greta, who often jokes she can only count to eight because she's also a musician. Maybe you've never used a spreadsheet. We understand, but we're going to walk you through it. The basics are easy. Honest.

First open a blank spreadsheet. Google Sheets is a great option—it's free and fairly self-explanatory. You could also use Excel or any other spreadsheet software you have access to. We don't recommend a word document, however, even if you add in a table. Dedicated spreadsheet software is much easier for this purpose.

At the top of the spreadsheet, create five columns: Cost Category, Vendor, Estimated Cost, Amount Paid, and Notes.

Now let's consider your expenses. What is your publisher going to do? What do you have to do? Who are you going to hire? (See Chapter One and Chapter Two) How much do these people charge? Are you able to trade services?

Here are some examples for your consideration:

General business expenses:

- Website domain
- Business cards
- Newsletter service

General manuscript preparation:

- Developmental Editor
- Copy Editor
- Proofreader
- Print copies to send to readers/editors

- Postage and shipping supplies to send print copies

Book production:
- Cover design
- Formatting
- ISBN purchase
- Paperback proof copies

Marketing:
- Promotional Materials (Bookmarks, postcards, swag, etc.)
- Website design
- Digital imagery (Social media banners, teaser images, etc.)
- Advertising (newsletter promotions like BookBub, Facebook ads, PR assistance, etc.)
- Giveaways (print copies, shipping, digital gifted copies)

Cushion:
- Make sure you pad your budget for surprises. There's always something you've forgotten or something that costs more than you thought it would. Prepare for the unexpected.

Once you have all your categories listed, fill in vendor names and estimated costs. At the bottom, create a sum for your total expenses. This is how much money you need to start production. Is it higher than you expected? Think through everything again and find places to cut costs. Is it lower than expected? Lucky!

As you hire and pay vendors, fill in the Amount Paid column. Were you able to find savings? Great. Did you go over budget in an area? Where can you make that back?

The notes column is for any exceptions or oddities that

occurred during the production phase. Was your cover designer late? Note that. Did the cover designer give you a discount because you booked the covers for your short story prequel and companion novella at the same time? Note that.

A budget is a living document, not a commandment written in stone. Revisit your budget at least once a month to make sure things are going as planned. If not, make changes.

We've included a template spreadsheet in Appendix 2 and in the Pro-Author Packet as examples for your overall book budget, and for the specific marketing costs you plan to invest in for your launch. Use these templates as a guide when thinking through your own expenses and setting up your own spreadsheets. You can download the digital packet for free when you join our community at www.AuthorWheel.com/ProAuthor.

TO RECAP

Set SMART Goals for publishing

- Specific
- Measurable
- Attainable
- Realistic
- Time-bound

Create a Calendar

- Break your big goal into manageable steps
- Plot those steps on your calendar
- Create a Budget
- Download our sample budget
- Fill it out and visit it regularly

Chapter Eight
Author Platform Basics

According to publishing expert Jane Friedman, an author platform is "an ability to sell books because of who you are or who you can reach."[7] An author platform is how you become visible to readers and engage with your target audience.

Developing an author platform is essential for building your author career, but it can be expensive in both time and resources. How many hours do you spend whiling away time on social media, writing blog posts instead of novels, or fiddling with the settings on your website?

Publicity—or public attention—always costs you something, even when it's free. So how do you decide which opportunities to jump on, and which ones to say no to? These are decisions you're going to have to make, but we can help you narrow it down a little. Much of your platform building depends upon the author personalities you learned about in the first chapter of this book. Let's go through them one by one:

AUTHOR PERSONALITY PLATFORM NEEDS

The Artist – You may want to focus your time solely on

your craft, but if you also want to sell your work, a functioning platform is an essential tool for you. Agents and publishers often want to see that you have some online savvy before they sign you. They only make money when or if you make money, so the fact that you're taking this author thing seriously will make you more attractive to them.

The minimum tools for the Artist are:

- An author website
- A newsletter or mailing list sign-up form
- A professional email account
- One or two active social media pages

The Bucket-Lister – If you only have one book in you, and your primary intention for that book is to give it to friends and family, you don't need much of an online presence. Whatever social media accounts you already use will suffice. However, if you actually hope to make sales or plan to build a business around the book, you'll want to create a website and mailing list as well.

The minimum tools for the Bucket-Lister are:

- One or two social media pages where you can connect with friends and family

The Calling-Card Writer – If your book supports your existing business, you probably already have a website, email list, and social media pages. If this is the case, simply adding a landing page to your website with information about the book and links to the stores where readers can purchase it is all you need.

The minimum tools for the Calling-Card Writer are:

- A landing page on existing website
- A newsletter or mailing list sign-up form
- A professional email account
- One or two active social media pages

The Dabbler – Hopefully by this point in the book you

have some direction, but if not don't despair. The bottom line is, if you want to make money from any form of writing whether it's freelance articles, marketing copy, selling short stories to anthologies, or long form books, you'll need an online presence. Our suggestion is to create a website under your name—not a business name—so you can easily adapt it as you grow and change.

Greta learned this the hard way. Her first website was under her business name, Fitness Inside Out, because she was a personal trainer. Her only published book at the time was *The Wine and Chocolate Workout*. When she left the fitness industry, she had to buy GretaBoris.com and start from scratch. If she'd started with GretaBoris.com, she could have had a page dedicated to *The Wine and Chocolate Workout* and blog posts about health and fitness, but also the flexibility to pivot.

The minimum tools for the Dabbler are:

- A website under their writer name
- One or two social media pages

The Entrepreneur – If your primary goal is to make a full-time income as a writer, you absolutely need an online presence. Since you are also business focused, choosing a website theme that has e-commerce capability, can showcase multiple books and/or series, and has a blog may be beneficial. You will also need a sign up form for your newsletter, a professional email service, and social media accounts wherever your future readers hang out.

The minimum tools for the Entrepreneur are:

- A flexible website
- An email list sign-up form
- A professional email account
- One or two active social media pages

WEBSITE MECHANICS

Some years ago it became popular for authors to use their Facebook pages as their online hub. Many spent time and money wooing followers, only to find they couldn't reach them without paying for advertising when Facebook changed their rules.

Think of your author brand as your home. It's where you live. Social media pages are like rental property. They're great until your landlord decides to sell or increase your rent. Websites, while they may cost more upfront, belong to you. If you're serious about writing, it's worth the investment. Then you can use the social media sites exactly as they're intended—social gathering places where you can meet and greet, but you'll always return home at the end of the day.

The good news is your website doesn't have to be complicated, and you don't have to spend hundreds or thousands of dollars hiring a web developer. You can do everything on your own in just a few simple steps.

Your first task is to choose a website building company. There are quite a few free and low-cost companies to choose from. WordPress is one of the most popular, and you can start there with a free site template. It's a very flexible and powerful system. Some find it complicated and unwieldy. Others love it. If you aren't afraid of a technical challenge, check them out.

Other website builders like Wix and Squarespace have out-of-the-box options. You won't need a lot of design experience to create a beautiful site. However, they're typically not as flexible or customizable as WordPress. The template may limit or restrain your design. It's also more difficult to add custom HTML. If the words "custom HTML" make your eyes glaze over, these companies could be perfect for you.

Most website builders have free trial periods, so do a little research, then pick one or two to test out. Once you find a program you like, it's time to choose a template and go to work.

A good template, or theme, is clean, clear, and easy for the reader to navigate. You'll be able to customize colors, images, and written content to suit your style and books. As you play with the settings, keep your target audience in mind—what colors and images will attract them? What are they looking for when they visit your site? What can you offer to pique their interest?

If you write horror, for example, you probably don't want rainbows and butterflies as featured images. If you write romance, you probably don't want dark backgrounds and corporate-looking fonts—unless, of course, you're writing a vampire romance with a CPA as the protagonist.

The key is to have fun and be creative. You can always switch themes later as your personal brand develops. Nothing is engraved in stone.

CHOOSE A DOMAIN NAME

Your next decision, the URL or address of your website, is more difficult to change down the road. Like a physical address, people learn where they can find you. If you alter that, you may lose followers.

It's best to own your domain. By which we mean, purchase a URL that doesn't have the hosting company's name in it. For example, Megan's website URL is MeganHaskell.com not megan-haskell.squarespace.com. Greta's is GretaBoris.com not greta-boris.wordpress.com. These addresses are easier to say out loud, easier to remember, and they're branded and therefore appear professional. And we can take them with us if we change hosting companies.

Your URL should be both easy to remember and uniquely related to your books. So mysterywriter.com, while easy to remember, could be anyone who writes mysteries. We suggest using your name or pen name. If someone has already taken your name, add "author" or "writes" or something similar to your name until you find an available URL.

We don't recommend fiction authors purchase a domain with their book or series title. After all, if you're a writer, you're going to write books and lots of them. It may be hard to imagine, but someday you may have fans. Super fans will read everything you write, whether it's action, adventure, or mystery. You can always have a page for each type of product, each book, or if you write multiple series, a page for each series.

Nonfiction authors can choose a URL that relates to their business, like Greta's FitnessInsideOut.com. Using your book title is also okay, but only if you plan to write one book and no more.

Finally, get a Dot Com domain, if at all possible. These are the easiest for readers to remember. Vanity domains, like .fun or .irish may be cute, but they don't stick in people's minds. For the same reason, avoid dashes. For example, if your name is Jane Doe, but www.janedoe.com isn't available, avoid www.jane-doe.com. While a growing number of people don't actively type the domain into their browser but search Google instead, your domain will still be written on everything from business cards to the back of your book.

Many of the site building companies will offer a free custom URL when you upgrade to a paid version of their site. If that's the case, great! If not, you can purchase a domain at any of a number of domain registrars, including GoDaddy, Hover, BlueHost, Domains.com, or HostGator. Once you own the domain, your site building company will have instructions on how to associate it with your new website.

Now that you have your URL and have decided where you're going to park your website, you can move on to building your content.

WEBSITE CONTENT

Some pieces of a website are optional, some are absolutely necessary. An 'About' page with an author biography and a nice-looking picture of you is one necessity. If you're writing under a pen name for privacy reasons, you might use a logo or other representational graphic instead, but it should be used consistently across all your online profiles so that readers will associate it with you and your brand.

Another important component of an author's site is a page for each book and/or for each series if you have a large backlist. Book pages should include the cover image, description, a free sample or a selection of your best reviews, and links to buy your book. It's a good idea to write and gather information early, so you have what you need when you build your site.

To blog or not to blog? There are people who argue that every author should have a blog on their website. For nonfiction authors, this is excellent advice. You can write about your topic, share articles and insights into your research, develop a reputation as an expert in your field, and draw in a group of people interested in your subject.

Sometimes, you can even modify the blog posts themselves and turn them into a book—recipes, parenting, and writing craft authors have all done this, and some have become best sellers. Plus, you can do all of this before your book is published, giving your launch a boost from an audience prepped to hit that buy button as soon as the book is available.

The answer to the blogging dilemma isn't as clear-cut for fiction writers. Some authors have used blogs to great success. Andy Weir, author of mega bestseller *The Martian*, is a perfect example. He started writing sci-fi in his twenties and published his work to his own website. *The Martian* began as a serialized novel on his blog. He also shared his research and the steps he took to ensure accuracy.

His readers clamored for a single manuscript. He

self-published the book on Amazon. When sales soared, an agent approached him and ultimately sold the print rights to Crown Publishing Group, and on to the movie studios. In other words, he built his audience long before he signed a book deal.

Andy Weir's success isn't the norm. We don't recommend that you independently publish with the goal of getting an agent and a big publishing contract. Very few people have accomplished this, and of those that did, most did it by accident. However, if you're comfortable posting your work in serialized form for free, it's a model to consider.

Many fiction writers don't find blogging helpful, however. Megan wasn't comfortable posting an unedited serial because her books require a lot of plot editing after she's finished with the first draft. So when she started blogging, she wrote about her research, world building, and writing process. She stressed over what to post every month, struggled to find relevant content to draw in new readers, and didn't enjoy the process at all. Ultimately, she felt her time and energy were better spent writing her novels, rather than writing about her novels.

Ultimately, whether or not to blog is up to you. If you find it fun and feel it's helpful, then go for it. If not, don't stress. There are plenty of other ways to find readers. Even if you choose to forgo a personal blog, writing for magazines or websites that have a bigger following than you do can be a great way for new authors to get their names into the public arena. A short story published in a literary magazine is not just an audience builder; you might get paid, and it looks great on your resume.

There are many websites and blogs looking for content. Book bloggers want author interviews and guest posts. Websites for writers need how-to articles and advice on craft. Nonfiction authors could target blogs and websites in their topic area, and fiction authors can pursue genre-targeted fan sites.

Often, the compensation provided by other blogs and websites is a link back to your personal website or your published works. It's free publicity and can be a great way to build your credibility.

CONNECT WITH READERS

Once your website is up and running, it's time to think about reaching out to potential readers. You can connect through a monthly, bi-monthly, or weekly newsletter, on social media, or both, but first you must determine who your audience is.

The first step in that process is to discover your unique sales proposition. To do that, you'll want to ponder a few questions. What was your initial motivation for writing your book? Did you have a story you had to get off your chest? A point of view you wanted to express? Or did you do it just to see if you could?

Whatever your reason, it was most likely a personal one. When Greta began writing fiction, she took the advice to write what you know a bit too literally. Her first novel attempt was about a woman going through a midlife crisis a lot like her own, who walked around her Southern California neighborhood with her dog pondering her woes. At about the three-quarter mark, she realized nothing was happening, so she had the character run into a serial killer. It was pretty bad.

Our early stories are often cathartic in nature. This is fine. You can learn a lot from tackling the challenge of penning 70,000 to 80,000 words on roughly the same subject, whatever the subject is, even if it's yourself. However, once you've finished that manuscript, it's time to take a long, hard look at it.

If you've followed the advice about quality control in Chapter Three, you've had outside eyes on your work, you know your genre, and you've compared it to similar books that are doing well. That's a great start. Now, you must reverse your position and look at your book from a reader's perspective.

Most people read for either education, inspiration, entertainment, or some combination of those. What does your book do best? If you've written a Christian romance with characters who struggle to remain pure until marriage, you're most likely trying to inspire. If you've written a book about healthy living during a pandemic, you're educating. A cozy mystery featuring a detective who reads minds sounds pretty entertaining to me.

Ask yourself these questions:

- Why would a reader pick up your book?
- What about it would hold their attention?
- What's different about this book than similar titles already on the market?

Once you know your book's unique sales proposition, you can zero in on your target market. The best way to do this is with a newsletter. In fact, the number one asset an author has, outside of his or her books, is the newsletter mailing list. This is made up of people who have entrusted you with their email address because they enjoy your work and want to know more.

With a mailing list, you don't have to worry about whether Amazon will promote your book, or if Facebook will show your post to the people who like your page. In both cases, and any other social media you use, the platform controls your connection to your fans. But if you build your own list, you control everything. You own the list. Even if you change platforms, you can take your list with you.

There are several well-respected mailing list service providers to choose from. Perhaps the best known is Mailchimp, but there are at least a dozen others, including MailerLite, Aweber, Emma, and ActiveCampaign. Each of these has some level of free use, usually with a maximum number of subscribers and a few limitations on the features. For the most part, when you're just starting out, any of them will do. Choose the one you like and open an account. Set up a form for your fans to subscribe to your list. Spend some time experimenting with the features and familiarizing yourself with the layout. Create a test email and send it to yourself to see how it looks.

Just like with blogging, whatever you choose to do, whatever rules you put in place for your newsletter, it's important to set and fulfill reader expectations, maintain a consistent schedule, and engage with your readers. Your reader is first and foremost.

Social Media

There are those who say every author should be active on Facebook, or Twitter, or Instagram, or Pinterest, or Tumblr, or . . . you name it. The fact is, you could tweet and post twenty-four hours a day and not cover all the social media sites. What works for one author might not work for you. Moreover, each social media site attracts a different user.

When you're thinking about joining a new platform, there are a few major points to consider:

Do you enjoy it? If not, it's probably not going to work for you, and you should probably say no.

Is your target audience active on the platform? If yes, you might want to find a way to like it, even if you don't right now.

Is there an active writing community on the platform? Sometimes it's not about how many books you can sell today, but the connections you make which might lead to more sales down the road.

How will you make connections? Always remember, social media is just that—social. Whatever you choose to do, don't spam the interwebs with "buy my book" posts. Instead, use the networks to engage with fans and colleagues as a real, live person.

How much time do you really have to spend? Social media can be a significant time sink. The more platforms you engage on, the more time you'll be spending not working on your manuscript. You have to say no to something.

Sometimes it helps to look at what people a few steps ahead of you are doing. We always recommend that you. . .

Stalk Other Authors

Online. Professionally. Not in real life. Authors have been stalked in scary, real life ways. We're not advocating that.

Go back to the list of books you made in Chapter Three and find the bestsellers or award winners in your genre. Search those authors online. Like their Facebook pages. Sign up for their mailing lists. Read their website copy. What are they doing to connect with readers?

You may love some of what they're doing and some of it you may find offensive. You may relate to their marketing ideas, or you may not be able to imagine yourself doing those things. You may find, especially if they're really big names, they're not doing much of anything. Search and follow until you find a handful of authors who are using interesting techniques you can relate to.

We've both gotten many terrific ideas this way. One author Greta admires has a Facebook book club. Every month her people read a different author's book, and she has a live Q&A with that author. A couple of times a year, everybody reads one of her books. This author has discovered her readers want to connect with one another. They're a community-oriented bunch.

Another author Greta stalks has a cute nickname for his followers. He sends frequent newsletters with anecdotes and photos of his family, his personal life, and his writing process. His readers want to be his friend.

Greta loves the idea of the online book club, but it's too time intensive for her, and she's found her readers aren't that interested in joining a community of other Greta Boris readers. On the other hand, they do email her when she tells them things about her personal life and asks questions about theirs.

It's more important at this phase of the game that you come up with a "flavor" for your online presence than an exact method of connecting. Greta's flavor is friendly, and sometimes inspiring because that's what she, as a reader, responds to from other authors.

Create an Ideal Reader Profile

Another great way to understand your audience is to write directly to an invisible reader. Somewhere in the process of revising *A Margin of Lust* with her editor, Greta began tweaking dialog and changing story lines with the editor's face (and her red pen) in her mind. Greta began to understand what Matrice liked, and what she didn't. Greta wanted to please. Suddenly her reader had a name—Matrice. It changed everything.

When she began book two in the series, she understood the importance of writing for a reader. This time, instead of thinking about her editor, she used her imagination to create a new character, Rachel Reader. She imagined her lounging in her backyard with a glass of wine, or cuddled by the fireplace with a cup of tea. Oh, and Greta's book.

And guess what? She couldn't put it down. Greta tweaked dialog and changed story lines to keep her riveted. She put her protagonist through the wringer, but threaded in moments of humor and warmth in the hopes Rachel would keep coming back for more.

The dog didn't die in act two, he just got very sick—Rachel wouldn't like a dead dog. But someone stalked the protagonist through a dark parking lot—which kept Rachel awake and turning pages.

If you make your reader as real as any of your characters, you can write to please her. When the book is done, you'll intuitively know what kind of cover she'd prefer and what types of author events she'd be tempted to attend.

Now it's your turn. Imagine Rachel or Ryan Reader and ask yourself these questions about them.

- Age?
- Level of education?
- Career or job?
- Married?
- Hobbies?
- Pet owner? (Pets are big in Greta's community. She has dogs in all her stories and they're some of her readers' favorite characters. They even send her pictures of their pets.)
- City, suburbs, or rural area?
- Favorite music genre?
- Favorite restaurant?
- Make and model of vehicle?
- Siblings?
- Relationship with parents?
- Favorite TV show?
- Other authors they enjoy?
- How would they like to connect with those authors?
- Which social media platforms are they on?
- What kind of newsletter would catch their attention?
- How frequently would they like to receive it?
- What kind of questions would they respond to?

Armed with this information, you can begin experimenting. Dialing in the perfect social media page or the perfect newsletter will take time. There will be trial and error, but now you have a starting point. You can write to Rachel or Ryan.

TO RECAP

Each Author Personality has different platform needs.

Website Mechanics

- Choose a website building company
- Choose a theme (template)
- Find your URL
- Decide on your website content

Connect with Readers

- Discover your unique sales proposition
- Start a mailing list and newsletter
- Choose one or two social media platforms
- Stalk other authors
- Create an ideal reader profile

Chapter Nine
Keep Your Stories Rolling

Once your book is published or on its way, it's time to look at your goals again. Was this a single passion project? Or did you fall in love with writing and publishing? Do you want to continue on this journey?

For some of you, this might be the end. Be proud of the work you've accomplished. You've met your big goal. Celebrate!

For others, this might be the first step. You may have read this book wanting a career as an author, or found your passion through the process. Either way, pop a bottle of champagne to celebrate the success of your first venture, then look to the future.

To be a writer means you have to keep writing.

There is an interesting TED Talk by psychologist Angela Lee Duckworth.[8] Ms. Duckworth and her team studied achievement. Their goal was to isolate predictors of success in all kinds of circumstances. They researched students, business professionals, athletes, people in many walks of life and varieties of endeavors. They found the individuals most likely to succeed all had one quality in common—grit. Ms. Duckworth defines grit as a combination of passion and persistence.

This is something every writer needs in abundance. We

don't think it's possible to imagine a piece of work, push past self-doubt to get it written, face the surgery of editing, the labor pains of the publishing process and the arrows of public scrutiny without grit. When a cashier job at Costco seems both less difficult and more lucrative, what else will keep us at the keyboard?

At this point in the book, we'd like to hit the pause button on all the busyness of the publishing process and talk about you, your mindset, your home office, and your organizational skills.

There are three kinds of writers: dreamers, doodlers, and authors. The dreamers won't face reality. Their aim is overnight success, and it often shows in both the quality of their work and their longevity. The doodlers have so little self-esteem or courage their stories never see the light of day.

And then there are authors.

Authors understand there is a road ahead of them and it won't be easy. They know they are going to lose their way, get mired in the mud, and run out of gas occasionally. They plan, they sweat, they swear, but they go the distance. They have grit. The question then is, how do we get grittier?

The publishing process is difficult on many fronts. It's hard practically, and it's hard emotionally. In some cases, it's hard financially as well. Sometimes life impedes our writing. Sometimes we face creative challenges, a lack of inspiration, or a lack of focus. We learn we can't wait for the muse to arrive, or for the stars to align. The perfect time to write is whatever time we can find.

Success isn't guaranteed, but those that succeed have common attitudes and behaviors.

TENACITY

A tenacious person is determined—unwilling to give up their dreams. A tenacious person is steadfast. They grab a hold of something and don't let go. As creative people who desire to be published, tenacity must become a part of who we are.

However, it's easier said than done. Wouldn't it be nice if there was a to-do list that would turn us into tenacious people as we ticked off the boxes? Maybe there is. Read on.

Have you ever heard of the Seinfeld Strategy? There's a story about a young comedian, Brad Isaac, who slipped backstage after a show one day and asked Jerry Seinfeld, arguably the most successful comedian on the planet, if he had any advice. Here's what Brad had to say about the encounter:

"He told me to get a big wall calendar that has a whole year on one page and hang it on a prominent wall. The next step was to get a big red magic marker.

He said for each day that I do my task of writing, I get to put a big red X over that day. 'After a few days you'll have a chain. Just keep at it and the chain will grow longer every day. You'll like seeing that chain, especially when you get a few weeks under your belt. Your only job is to not break the chain.'"

Don't break the chain. That's it. Tenacity in a nutshell. But how do we do that? What do we need to do to keep that chain going?

An article posted to creativity website 99U entitled "5 Scientific Ways to Build Habits That Stick: Eliminate 'ah-screw-its' and other ways to make that new habit last for the long haul"[10] had some interesting things to say. In their estimation, the number one method to make and keep a habit was to create "micro quotas" and "macro goals." What does that mean?

If you've been reading this book chronologically, then you should have already identified your macro goals. You've chosen your preferred path to publication, and you've created a basic project plan or timeline to help get you there. Micro quotas are the smallest daily tasks needed to move you forward.

To make this example simple, let's talk about the universal goal for any writer: the completion of a first draft. You have your deadline, right? The date that the first draft needs to be finished so you can send it off to your editor or beta readers or critique group. Now, how many words per day do you need to write to finish that draft by that day? That number could be your micro quota. Or you might need to think even smaller.

Megan isn't a fast writer. At least, not yet. She wants to get faster, however, so one day she challenged herself with a short deadline. To complete her eighty-thousand word manuscript by that date, she needed to write about fifteen hundred words per working day. Why not try?

Fifteen hundred words was a stretch for her. A significant challenge. Keeping that up over many consecutive days became a monumental task. If she missed a day, she became demotivated. Or she would reassure herself that she would "make it up tomorrow." However, that meant she'd need to write three thousand words the next day, or forty-five thousand the day after, and so on.

Soon she was totally overwhelmed, stressed out, and defeated. If she didn't make a change, she would not only miss her self-imposed deadline, she might quit writing the book altogether. Not acceptable.

Megan had to change her mindset. Instead of demanding enormous accomplishments from herself, she set an impossible-not-to-achieve micro quota: to work on her manuscript every day. She could write one sentence, or five thousand words. She could spend ten minutes at her desk, or two hours. But she must work on the manuscript *every single day*.

What kind of progress can be achieved with such low standards? You'd be amazed. Setting the habit of sitting down to work every day increased her productivity. In the beginning there were plenty of days she was happy to get a hundred words on the page. Fifty. But every time she did, she got the dopamine hit that comes with success.

Within a week or two, her averages improved. Soon it was easy to sit down and write. Her brain and fingers learned what she expected of them. Eventually, she was regularly exceeding her original fifteen-hundred word goal.

Did she miss some days? Of course. She wasn't perfect. But when she did, she picked herself up and started fresh the next day. After all, she only had to write something, anything, to get her dopamine fix.

Start with the simplest micro quota leading to your macro goal: work on your manuscript every day for five days in a row. Use a red pen to cross out the days you write on your calendar. Don't break the chain. Then celebrate. You're starting a new habit and becoming a gritty writer.

CONTRACTS

Successful business people know the importance of contracts. Many fortunes have been lost or made by them. A good contract is clear, detailed, and takes all contingencies into account.

Unfortunately, creative endeavors can be hard to pin down and in the beginning no one is asking us to. Sure, we all want to be writers. We all want to be successful. We *say* we're determined to make a full-time income from our books, but when the road to financial success looks like a cross-country trek, it's easy to make a pit stop and get lost along the way.

How do we keep going when no one cares? How do we forge ahead in the face of rejection? How do we stay focused on the finish line when it looks like a mirage in the distance?

There is a wonderful book called *The War of Art* by Steven Pressfield, who's a successful novelist and screenplay writer. In it he proposes that as soon as you do *anything* positive, anything life-altering, anything that will break you out of the humdrum, repetitive rat-race of your life, you are going to run into Resistance. Note, it's spelled with a capital R.[11]

Pressfield outlines many weapons against Resistance. Knowing it exists and is on its way is a start. Another Resistance-defeating strategy is to sign a contract with yourself. As we stated before, in the early days of your writing life nobody cares if you meet your goals. In fact, sometimes friends and family will sabotage you. There is only one person who has your best interests at heart in this endeavor, you.

We suggest you take a day, or a week, to think through your business plan. List the things you will do to see your book in print, and the things you won't. Count the costs in time, money, and emotions. Then write a clear, detailed contract that takes as many contingencies as you can think of into account. Once you're in agreement with yourself, sign it. Then be a man or woman of your word.

Finally, Resistance has a hard time standing up to Humility. Understanding the importance of books and stories without allowing your self-importance to inflate can be difficult. On one hand, we believe writers provide the ingredients for the soup of the future. If it weren't for Alfred Hitchcock, *The Twilight Zone,* and *Star Trek,* where would we be today? Some of those stories probably paved the way for iPhones, laptops, and *CSI.* We're sure we heard somewhere Steve Jobs was a Trekkie. What tomorrow brings comes from the minds of today.

But no matter how critical our industry is, we must see ourselves as a part, not a superstar. The reality is you may have to write ten books to find the one that alters thought, and you may never achieve that. You will write silly stories that don't cut it. We have. You will write drivel. We've done that, too. You will write redundancies. Hand raised. But in the trying, you might write genius. You never know.

You might be the one who inspires an engineer or inventor,

politician or preacher, explorer or archaeologist to change the world.

It's freeing to recognize it really isn't about you. It isn't about your success, or your Amazon reviews. It is about the spark your story might ignite. It may take fifteen books before one strikes the match, but once it's struck, what fires can be lit? Your mission is much more than pleasing New York publishers and snarky Goodreads reviewers. Your mission is to help others live vicariously.

One of the best ways we know of to gain perspective is to . . .

WRITE THE NEXT BOOK

There are many positive things that happen when we write more books. Our first attempts are near and dear to our hearts. Writing them, seeking publication or planning to publish ourselves is an emotion-packed journey. Not only that, but we're waiting with bated breath to see if our creation will be received into the ranks of successful books. We see it as a referendum on our writing ability, our creativity, our potential, and our future.

We're not objective about our first book. To be honest, we probably won't be completely objective about our second, or our third, or our fiftieth either, but we do get more objective when we have a body of work.

We also become better writers. The first time you do anything is the most difficult. Think about all those home improvement projects that took you three times longer than it would take a professional to do. Writing a book is no different. By the time you type the words "The End" you know a lot more than you did in the first chapter. This is true every time. We've both learned something new with every book we've written.

The more books we write and publish, the more insight into our audience we have. When a book is on the market, you'll begin getting reviews. Sometimes they're on Amazon or Goodreads, sometimes they're verbalized around the dinner table. Either way, if you keep an open mind they'll teach you what you did right and what you could improve on.

The more we write, the bigger our vision becomes. Greta couldn't imagine where writers got all their ideas before she started writing. She isn't alone in this. It's the most common question writers are asked at book signing events.

Here's the truth. Often authors find that somewhere at about the half-way point in whatever book they're writing they hit the saggy middle, the place things get really hard. It's in that spot they get a crazy good idea for another book. Call it escapism, or optimism, or whatever you like, but the more you write, the more the ideas will flow.

And finally, writing more books means we are career authors. Yes, once your first book is published you can call yourself an author, but career authors write books. Lots of them. Even calling-card writers often realize they have more to say than their first book says.

Singers sing. Dancers dance. Artists paint. And writers write. Don't fall into the trap of thinking that if your first book doesn't get picked up, or doesn't sell well on Amazon, it's a cosmic sign that you should give up. It isn't. It may be a sign you need to take another writing course, or read another book on craft. It may mean there is a heck of a lot of competition out there, and this whole author thing is going to take longer than you thought. Or, it might mean you need to write your next book.

What should you write next?

Before we answer that question, let's talk about what maybe you shouldn't write. Writers are readers first. As a reader, you probably enjoy many genres, and that's great. The more widely you read, the more interesting your books will be. However, it isn't always the best strategy from a marketing perspective to write in multiple genres for many reasons.

The first is that it's time intensive to grow an audience. The more genres you write in, the more different reader groups you must appeal to. The people who enjoy your sci-fi novel aren't the target market for your romance series.

Writing in two or more genres and using the same author name will risk confusing readers, thus you'll need a pen name. For every pen name you use, you must replicate your platform building. Each name should have its own website, mailing list, social media sites, etc . . .

As you can see, genre-hopping may scratch your creative itch, but it's time and labor intensive. Once you have a raving fan base, you might segue from one subgenre to a related one. For instance, Nora Roberts writes romance, and romantic suspense, and supernatural stories with strong romantic elements. Not all of her readers will like all three, but they are similar enough to create crossover.

Her murder mysteries are written under a completely different pen name, J.D. Robb, because they appeal to a completely different audience. Nora Roberts can do that. She has an entire marketing team at her disposal. She's a superstar. We aren't there yet.

Enough on what you shouldn't do. Let's talk about what you should do. Series are popular in fiction because they not only sell books, they help authors build a fan base. People want to know if they invest time in a story, get attached to the characters, or the world, that there will be more to come. How can you turn your stand-alone novel into a series?

Greta took a class from romance author Lisa Wells on writing a series. According to Lisa, there are four basic types: the really big book, the linked sequential, the linked stand-alone, and the loosely connected stand-alone.[12]

An example of the really big book series would be the *Lord of the Rings* trilogy by Tolkien. Book one begins Frodo's story, book two continues it and book three wraps it up. If it wouldn't break your arm to hold, the entire trilogy could be one really big book.

Jan Karon's *Mitford* series is an example of a linked sequential series. In this series, there is an overarching storyline that moves from book to book. If you read them out of order, you will wonder who certain characters are and when so and so got married. But each novel also has a plot of its own that wraps up at its end.

The linked stand-alone series is the most popular of the mystery and crime genres. Think Agatha Christie's *Miss Marple* books, or Lee Child's *Jack Reacher* series. Each story is complete. We can read them out of order. What links them is the protagonist.

Finally, there are the loosely connected stand-alone novels. In these, each story is complete and has its own protagonist. What connects them is the world, and the cast of characters. An example of this is Tana French's *Murder Squad* books. All her protagonists work for the Irish Murder Squad. Each story is a separate case, solved by its own detective, but the detectives are connected through the world she has created.

How do you choose which series is right for you? Certain genres lend themselves to certain series types. Fantasy, especially high fantasy, is perfect for the big book series because often the author is telling the story of a world, or an epic journey with a huge cast of characters. It's a history of sorts.

The linked sequential series is a natural for following a character through the stages of life, or for a family epic. Linked stand-alone novels are a perfect foil for the quirky detective.

Greta chose to write loosely connected stand-alone books for her *Seven Deadly Sins* series. She likes domestic suspense, and by definition domestic suspense occurs when something bizarre happens to Joe Blow Average. The plots revolve around the idea that a normal person—not a cop, or an ex-Navy Seal, or a crime reporter—stumbles into a life or death situation.

Since thrillers need to be tight stories with a ticking clock going in the background, neither of the first two types of series made sense. She also couldn't have a real estate agent (the protagonist in book one) bumping into serial killers every other month, so that ruled out the third. There was only one option left.

Nonfiction writers can also write a series. Think about the *Chicken Soup for the Soul* books—which were a bit of marketing genius even if they aren't great literature. There is a Chicken Soup for the Busy Mom, the Golfer, the Dog Lover. You name it, if you can categorize a person into a sub-group there is a *Chicken Soup for the Soul* book for them.

Take a hard look at your book. Does it have series potential? Can you write a spin off? Is it long enough to divide into three books? Or could your next book, like Tolkien's *The Hobbit*, be a prequel to a series?

We know writing and publishing a book can be an exhausting process. We highly suggest a European vacation, a trip to the beach, or at least a nap when you're done. But after the celebration, we hope we have inspired you to pick yourself up, dust yourself off, and start your next book.

TO RECAP

Get gritty:

- Build tenacity through micro-quotas that lead to macro goals
- Defeat Resistance with a solid self-contract

Writing more books has positive effects:

- We become more objective about our work
- We become better writers
- We gain insight into our audience

- We get a bigger vision
- We have a career

Types of book series:

- The Really Big Book Series
- The Linked Sequential Series
- The Linked Standalone Series
- The Loosely Connected Standalone Series
- Nonfiction for different populations

Final Thoughts

Millions of people dream of writing a book. Most won't ever set word to page, let alone write, edit, and publish one.

If you've read this book from beginning to end, you're likely one of the few who have . . . or will.

The journey may be long and winding. The path may be overgrown with weeds. You may find the shortcut was really a scenic byway. Your journey will be unique, no matter what you choose to do.

We hope that we've given you the means to reach your goals, and the encouragement to keep on going. If you found it was all too much, then at least you've checked a powerful item off your bucket-list. But if you've fallen in love with writing and publishing . . . Welcome to the madhouse.

PUBLISH: Take Charge of Your Author Career...
THE COURSE

If you'd like to take a deeper dive into the material presented in this book, consider enrolling in our course on Udemy. With over three hours of downloadable video lectures, detailed action plans, and the ability to ask us questions directly, we'll help you keep your stories rolling.

For more information, visit our website at www.AuthorWheel.com/PublishCourse.

And don't forget to download your free Pro-Author Packet with the template spreadsheets, questionnaire, and more at www.AuthorWheel.com/ProAuthor.

Appendix 1
Service Providers and Online Resources

Service Providers Used in the Creation of this Book:

Kimberly Peticolas
Editor & Interior Formatting
www.KimPeticolas.com

Are you an indie author in need of an editor and publishing guide? Pursuing traditional publication, but looking for extra help to snag the agent of your dreams? What about a small business looking for assistance with publishing projects? Kimberly Peticolas can help you with all your publishing needs.

Kimberly Peticolas is an experienced editor, writing coach, and publishing consultant working with clients from a variety of backgrounds. No matter your publishing goals, she's here to help you achieve your writing dreams. With *á la carte* services ranging from one-on-one author coaching to detailed manuscript editing and proofreading, or even extra help to improve your writing skills, Kimberly has you covered.

Check www.kimpeticolas.com for current rates and available services.

OTHER RESOURCES

Places to find literary agents or boutique publishers online:
- Agent Query
- Carissa Taylor: Pitch Contest Calendar
- Duotrope
- Jane Friedman – How to find a Literary Agent
- Publisher's Marketplace
- Querytracker
- Savvy Authors
- Writer's Market

Taglines & Queries:
- Margie Lawson Writer's Academy
- Query Shark
- Writers Helping Writers

(Also check the agent websites you might be interested in. Many of them have blogs where they talk about what grabs them in a query, and what doesn't.)

Writing conferences – where to find them:
- Association of Writers and Writing Programs – Conference Database
- New Pages – Writing Conferences and Events
- Writers and Editors – Conferences, Workshops and Other Learning Places

National genre based organizations:

- Historical Writers of America
- Horror Writers of America
- International Thriller Writers
- Mystery Writers of America
- Romance Writers of America
- Science Fiction and Fantasy Writers of America
- Sisters in Crime
- Society of Children's Book Writers and Illustrators

Setting up a website:

- Getting Started with WordPress
- New to WordPress – Where to Start
- Getting Started with SquareSpace
- Getting Started with Wix

Appendix 2
Beta Reader Questionnaire &
Template Spreadsheets

Digital downloads of these templates and more are available FREE when you join our community at www.AuthorWheel.com/proauthor.

Beta Reader Questionnaire

Below is a template letter that you can modify for your own use. Be careful to make sure that it matches your books and requirements!

Dear [NAME],

Thank you so much for volunteering to be a beta reader. Your feedback is critical to bringing out the best in this story. Without readers like you, I wouldn't be the writer that I am today!

If you've been a beta reader before, whether for me or for other writers, you know that constructive criticism is crucial for the editing process. You may love a story, but saying "It's great" doesn't help the author make it even better. Nor does "I hated it."

I need to know why.

This questionnaire is designed to help you think critically about the book as you read. For that reason, please read through the questions before you begin the book so you know what kind of information I'm looking for.

This list is long. You do not have to answer every single question, but the questions are intended to prompt a critical reading, and help generate the constructive criticism that will guide the next revision of the book. Please feel free to pick and choose from the list in whatever way feels appropriate for you.

I have created a Google Form to collect your responses to the questions. This makes it easier for me to understand the overall response of the group as well as review each individual answer. You can access the form here: [INSERT YOUR LINK]

Once again, thank you so much for volunteering to be a beta reader.

Sincerely,
[YOUR NAME]

**Questions to be answered via the Google Form Here:
[INSERT YOUR LINK]**

Initial Thoughts

1. Was the opening compelling? At what point did you first stop reading? Why?

2. Was there a point (after the first chapter or two) at which your interest increased or decreased significantly?

3. On a scale of 1 to 5, how engaged were you in the story? If your interest fluctuated, can you tell me where and why? (1 = I only barely managed to finish reading it, and then only because I promised you I would, 5 = I couldn't stop reading, found myself neglecting household chores and family members to keep going.)

4. How was the pace of the novel? Were there any sections that moved too fast or too slow?

5. What were your favorite scenes/chapters/sections of the novel? Why?

6. What scenes/chapters/sections of the novel did you not like? Why?

7. Did any scenes give you a physical reaction? (e.g. laugh out loud, heart race, cringe, cry, etc.)

8. Did any scenes/paragraphs/lines resonate or move you emotionally?

9. How did you feel about the book's climax and resolution? Was it satisfying?

Consistency and Continuity

10. Did you notice any inconsistencies in the plot, setting, character descriptions, or dialogue?

11. Did you notice any gaps in the story, sections where you wanted more information or felt like something was missing?

12. Were there any noticeable plot holes or jumps in logic?

13. Was there anything that confused or frustrated you?

Craft

14. Did the setting pull you in, and did the descriptions seem vivid and real to you?

15. Did you ever feel there was too much description? Not enough?

16. Did you ever feel there was too much dialogue? Not enough?

17. Did the dialogue sound natural (for the character)? If not, whose dialogue did you think sounded artificial, and where in the story?

18. Were the characters three-dimensional and believable? Did you feel there were any that needed further development?

19. Did you feel connected to the characters?

20. Did you notice any overused words, phrases, or body language descriptions?

21. Were there any sections/ideas/backstory that felt too long and should be compressed?

22. Were there any sections/ideas/backstory where you wanted more (e.g. more backstory, deeper emotions, etc).

Final Thoughts

23. What is the novel's greatest strength?

24. What is the novel's biggest weakness?

25. Any other comments or suggestions?

Book Production Budget - Traditional

This template can be used as a general guide to the types of expenses you might incur as a traditional author. Consider this spreadsheet a starting point: add or substract line-items as necessary. Try to think through all of your expenses before you begin paying vendors, and revisit this budget periodically to make sure you're staying on track.

Category	Item	Vendor	Estimated Cost	Actual Paid	Difference (Estimated - Actual)	Notes
General Business Expenses	Website Domain & Hosting					
	Website Design					
	Newsletter Service					
	Business Cards					
	Total - General Business Expenses		0	0	0	
Manuscript Preparation	Developmental Edit					
	Copy-Edit					
	Total - Manuscript Preparation		0	0	0	
Marketing	Advertising					
	Giveaways					
	Promotional Materials					
	Total - Advertising and Promotion		0	0	0	
Cushion	Cushion					
Total Costs			0	0	0	

Book Production Budget - Independent

This template can be used as a general guide to the types of expenses you might incur as an independent author. Consider this spreadsheet a starting point: add or substract line-items as necessary. Try to think through all of your expenses before you begin paying vendors, and revisit this budget periodically to make sure you're staying on track.

Category	Item	Vendor	Estimated Cost	Actual Paid	Difference (Estimated - Actual)	Notes
General Business Expenses	Website Domain & Hosting					
	Website Design					
	Newsletter Service					
	Business Cards					
	Total - General Business Expenses		0	0	0	
Manuscript Preparation	Developmental Edit					
	Copy-Edit					
	Formatting					
	Proofreader					
	Cover					
	ISBN					
	Proofs					
	Total - Manuscript Preparation		0	0	0	
Marketing	Digital Imagery					
	Advanced Review Copies					
	Advertising					
	Giveaways					
	Promotional Materials					
	Total - Marketing		0	0	0	
Cushion	Cushion					
Total Costs			0	0	0	

Marketing Budget Template

This template provides more detail on the types of marketing expenses you might accrue. You can use the total of each category as a line-item on the Book Production Budget.

Category	Item	Vendor	Estimated Cost	Actual Paid	Difference (Estimated - Actual)	Notes
Digital Imagery	3D Book Covers					0
	Advertising Images					0
	Teaser Images					0
	Total - Digital Imagery		0	0		0
Advanced Review Copies	eBook					0
	Paperback					0
	Total - Advanced Review Copies		0	0		0
Advertising	Paid Newsletter Promotion					0
	Facebook Ads					0
	Amazon Ads					0
	Total - Advertising		0	0		0
Giveaways	Paperbacks					0
	Postage					0
	Gift Cards					0
	Gifted eBooks					0
	Total - Giveaways		0	0		0
Promotional Materials	Bookmarks					0
	Postcards					0
	Other "Swag"					0
	Total - Promotional Materials		0	0		0
Total Marketing Expenses			0	0		0

Submission Tracker

This spreadsheet can be used to track your query letter submissions, review requests, or other requests for information. We suggest using a separate spreadsheet for each type of submission. For example, if you're querying multiple projects, you'll want a separate spreadsheet for each manuscript.

Agent/Editor Name	Company Name	Email Address	What Did You Send?	Date Sent	Time Frame	Response Date	Response	Notes	Follow up
Amelia Agent	Hard to Impress Agency	Amelia@HTIAgency	Query Letter & 10 Pages	8/18/18	6 months (or forget it)	10/10/18	Send Full!!!	She loved it. Will let me know about full by 1/30/19	

About the Authors

The Author Wheel Founders

Together, Greta Boris and Megan Haskell have more than twenty years of writing and publishing experience. We've made the mistakes, so you don't have to!

Greta Boris

Greta Boris is the USA Today Bestselling author of the 7 Deadly Sins Series from Fawkes Press. Ordinary women. Unexpected Evil. Taut psychological suspense novels that expose the dark side of sunny Southern California. Her books have been called atmospheric and un-put-down-able.
Email: Greta@GretaBoris.com

Megan Haskell

Megan Haskell is the award-winning author of The Sanyare Chronicles, a fast-paced dark fantasy adventure featuring a kick-ass heroine, snarky carnivorous pixies, and a quest across nine faerie realms. Sanyare: The Last Descendant (Book 1) received a Readers' Favorite Bronze Award and was a finalist in the 2017 IAN Book of the Year Awards, and Sanyare: The Rebel Apprentice (Book 3), was named a finalist in the 2018 Book Excellence Awards.
Email: Megan@MeganHaskell.com

Endnotes

1   Tracy Spears and Wally Schmader, "It's Time To Give Noel Burch Some Credit," Exceptional Leaders Lab, July 11, 2017, https://exceptionalleaderslab.com/its-time-to-give-noel-burch-some-credit/.

2   Adam Levenburg, "Official Screenwriting Podcast," Official Screenwriting, December 20, 2015, http://officialscreenwriting.com/category/the-official-screenwriting-podcast/.

3   "Harry Potter and the Sorcerer's Stone," IMDb (IMDb.com), accessed February 11, 2021, https://www.imdb.com/title/tt0241527/plotsummary.

4   VK Ranganathan et al., "From Mental Power to Muscle Power--Gaining Strength by Using the Mind," PubMed (National Library of Medicine, 2004), https://pubmed.ncbi.nlm.nih.gov/14998709/.

5   Leora Rifkin, "How to Stop Daydreaming and WOOP into Action," LifeLabs Learning, January 22, 2020, https://lifelabslearning.com/lab/woop/.

6   Stacey Hanke, "Write Your Professional Goals Into Reality," Forbes (Forbes Magazine, February 10, 2020), https://www.forbes.com/sites/forbescoachescouncil/2020/02/10/write-your-professional-goals-into-reality/?sh=6bdb43843a83.

7   Jane Friedman, "A Definition of Author Platform," Jane Friedman, September 17, 2020, https://www.janefriedman.com/author-platform-definition/.

8   Angela Lee Duckworth, "Grit: The Power of Passion and Perseverance," TED (TED Talks), accessed February 9, 2021, https://www.ted.com/talks/angela_lee_duckworth_grit_the_power_of_passion_and_perseverance.

9   Gina Trapani, "Jerry Seinfeld's Productivity Secret," Lifehacker (Lifehacker, June 25, 2013), http://lifehacker.com/281626/jerry-seinfelds-productivity-secret.

10   Gregory Ciotti, "5 Scientific Ways to Build Habits That Stick," Adobe 99U (Behance, Inc., February 26, 2019), http://99u.com/articles/17123/5-scientific-ways-to-build-habits-that-stick.

11   Steven Pressfield, The War of Art: Break Through the Blocks and Win Your Inner Creative Battles (New York, NY: Black Irish Entertainment, 2002).

12   Margie Lawson, "Getting Serious about Writing a Series," Margie Lawson, September 19, 2020, https://www.margielawson.com/getting-serious-about-writing-a-series/.